How to Be Sure You're Going to HEAVEN

MICHAEL TAYLOR

WESTBOW
PRESS®
A DIVISION OF THOMAS NELSON
& ZONDERVAN

WestBow Press books may be ordered through booksellers or by contacting:

WestBow Press
A Division of Thomas Nelson & Zondervan
1663 Liberty Drive
Bloomington, IN 47403
www.westbowpress.com
844-714-3454

ISBN: 978-1-5127-7026-1 (sc)
ISBN: 978-1-5127-7027-8 (hc)
ISBN: 978-1-5127-7025-4 (e)

Library of Congress Control Number: 2017901307

Print information available on the last page.

WestBow Press rev. date: 04/22/2021

This is dedicated

to all the men and women who, through the years,
have taught me the Scriptures;

to all those who have challenged my views, forcing me to
dig deeper into the Word of God to discover His truths;

to all those who have proofread, edited, and helped
in any way to publish this book;

and of course, to my Lord and Savior Jesus Christ
who has given me knowledge and wisdom.

Acknowledgments

I want to thank the following individuals
for their help, suggestions, and support
in the production of this book:

Barbara Moten
Anita Adger
Nathaniel Taylor
Holly Taylor
Timothy Bailey

Contents

Preface

A few years ago, I went to a hospital to visit a sick friend. Just by chance I decided to go into the hospital bookstore to see if I might find something that might be encouraging for my friend. To my surprise I didn't see any books at all. Magazines yes, but books, no. I was shocked to say the least, because you would think that at a hospital there would be all kinds of books written to offer encouragement. That's when the Lord gave me the idea to write this book, and I pray that He will use it.

I have two purposes for this book. First, I've written it in the hope that it will provide real encouragement to Christians who are sick, especially those who are terminally ill. Second, I've written this book for everyone else: because you see, in a sense, we are all terminally ill. We just don't know it yet.

Now, while it is true that everyone can learn something, and benefit from this book, I have obviously written it with Christians in mind. And I'm talking about "real" Christians – "born again Christians." This book has been written to encourage all of us, and to remind us that we are saved by grace through faith. Not by works. Oh, don't get me wrong, works are important. James said it best ". . . **faith without works is dead**" (Jam. 2:21). But good works can't save us. Nor can they help to keep us saved. Good works are the result of salvation. They are the proof, the real proof that we are saved. That's why Paul said . . .

"For by grace ye are saved through faith; and that not of yourselves: *it is* **the gift of God: not of works, lest anyone should boast. For we are His workmanship, created in Christ Jesus unto good works, which God has before ordained that we should walk in them"** (Eph. 2:8-10).

May the Lord Jesus bless you, and provide you real comfort, and real encouragement.

Michael

Are You Sure You're A Christian?

CHAPTER ONE

Are you sure you're a Christian? Are you sure you're saved? Are you really sure? . . . The reason why I ask is because through the years, I have talked with many many people who simply were not sure. What makes this truly tragic is that most of these individuals were people who attended church regularly. They were people who were active in church. And yet, they weren't sure.[1]

For example, some time ago I decided I would go back and visit the church I used to attend when I was a child. When the morning service was over I got an opportunity to speak with

---

[1] When I attended the University of Kansas I became involved with Campus Crusade for Christ. Then, after I graduated, I became a Staff Member, and was on staff for about two years. I say that because a lot of the material in this chapter is based on the teachings of Dr. Bill Bright in *Transferable Concept 1.* You can get all of the Transferable Concepts from New Life Resources. Cru, New Life Resources, 665 Highway 74 South, Suite 350, Peachtree City, GA. 30269.

1

many of my old friends whom I hadn't seen in years. While we were reminiscing about the good old days, I overheard one of the Deacons in the background say to another member, "Larry, I don't know if I'm going to heaven, but I sure am working on it." Now honestly, I wasn't trying to eavesdrop. I just happened to hear a part of his conversation. But I thought to myself, here is a man who has been a member of this church for 30 years, and he still thinks he has to do good works to get to heaven. Now, don't get me wrong, he was a good family man, and over the years he had been very active in the church. Yet, he wasn't sure he was saved.

Once, when I was in Daytona Beach, Florida, I led a student to Christ. After I shared the gospel with him he bowed, and prayed, and asked Jesus Christ to come into his life. Now, in order to make sure he knew he was a Christian, I asked him after he prayed, "Do you know that Christ is in your life?" He looked at me and said, "I don't know, I don't feel any different." Here, just a few moments ago, he had prayed and asked Christ to come into his life. And yet, he still wasn't sure if Christ had come in.

What's really bad though, is that I know of evangelists, pastors, preachers, and missionaries who experience this same tormenting uncertainty. A few years ago a local church was looking for a pastor. So they asked me if I would serve as the chairman of their Pastoral Search Committee. Well at the time I was young and naive, and I didn't know what I was getting myself into, so I accepted. While we earnestly looked and prayed for God to direct us to the man He wanted to lead the church, we ran across several ministers who didn't believe you could be sure of your salvation. One in particular told me there is no way a person can know for sure about their salvation. The only thing we can do is try to live a good life. When I asked him why he believed that he said, "Because you have to live right to get to heaven." I could not believe it! Here was a man who, I'm sure, had committed his life to saving others, and yet, he wasn't even sure about his own eternal destiny.

Why does this uncertainty exist among so many people who sincerely want to know God and spend eternity with Him? I am personally convinced that the lack of assurance is due either to a lack of information, or misinformation, concerning: who God is; the real purpose of the life, death, and resurrection of Jesus Christ; and, what is involved in becoming a Christian.

NO INFORMATION OR MISINFORMATION

If a person is not sure they are a Christian it is usually due to a lack of information. They may not know what a Christian is, or what is involved in becoming a Christian. You see, Christianity is not like other religions. It is not a philosophy, nor is it a set of moral principles; nor is it a system of dos and don'ts. Christianity is different! Because it is the only religion in which a person can actually have a relationship (a close friendship) with God! Now, there is only one way a person can have a relationship with God. They must receive Jesus. Therefore, a Christian is someone who has received Jesus Christ as their personal Lord and Savior.

Still others are unsure about their salvation because they have been misinformed. They believe that in order to be saved you have to live a good life, or obey the Ten Commandments, or become a member of a church, or get baptized, or perform good works: like selling your possessions and giving the money to the poor. But there is only one way a person can be sure they will spend eternity with God in heaven. Again, they must receive Jesus Christ.

Now because of this, the historical facts surrounding the birth, life, death, and resurrection of Jesus Christ are extremely important. Especially now, because Jesus prophesied that He would come back to judge and rule the world shortly after Israel became a nation again. Could it be that you are still unsure about your relationship with God, even though you may have been raised in a Christian home? Are you absolutely certain that you are a Christian? That you are a child of God? If you were terminally ill, and only had one month to live, do you know where you would spend eternity? Do you wonder from time to time about whether you will go to heaven or hell when you die, or are you confident you will live forever with God in heaven? If you are still not sure you're a Christian, it is my hope that by the end of this chapter you will be.

AN INTELLECTUAL UNDERSTANDING

In order to become a Christian, a person must first of all have a clear intellectual understanding of who Jesus Christ is. Christianity is not "a blind leap of faith." It is built upon documented historical facts. Many Christian scholars have spent their whole lives investigating the birth, life, death, resurrection, and influence of Jesus. As a matter of fact, many people who started out as non-Christians, seeking to disprove the life, miracles, death, and resurrection of Jesus have been converted to Christianity, because the documented facts are so overwhelming.[2] As a result, we now have more historical

---

[2] If you would like to investigate the historical facts documenting the birth, life, death, and resurrection of Jesus Christ, I would encourage you to read the following books. By the way, I believe all of these people originally set out to disprove Christianity, but in the end, they were all converted: Josh McDowell, *Evidence That Demands A Verdict* (San Bernardino, CA: Here's Life Publishers, Inc., 1979); Stan Telchin, *Betrayed!* (Old Tappen,

proof of Christ's life, death, and resurrection than we have of Custer's last stand.

For instance, we know that Jesus was born in 4 B.C.; He lived in Nazareth, and had brothers and sisters (well actually, half brothers and half sisters), and, we know when He was crucified – in 30 A.D. We also know that when Jesus' dead body was taken off the cross it was mummified. His followers wrapped His corpse with long strips of linen cloth. And spices were placed in between the strips to act as a sort of glue, and, provide a fragrant aroma to help take the stench away.

Scholars have also discovered that Jesus' tomb was actually a cave. After Jesus was buried a large stone, weighing about two tons, was placed over its opening. The tomb was also guarded by approximately 16 trained soldiers, and a Roman Seal was placed on the tomb.[3] All of this was done to prevent anyone from stealing the body. Yet despite all this, Jesus' tomb was empty early Sunday morning! Jesus Christ actually rose from the dead!

That good news was the revolutionary message of the first century church. And it is still a revolutionary message today. Jesus Christ rose from the dead! It's a fact of history. Listen to the words of Paul the apostle. He writes, **"brethren, I declare unto you the gospel . . . which I also received, how that Christ died for our sins according to the Scriptures; and that He was buried, and that He rose again *on* the third day according to the Scriptures: and that He was seen by**

NJ: Chosen Books, 1981); and Frank Morison, *Who Moved The Stone* (London: Faber and Faber, 1958).

[3] An official Roman seal, probably made of wax or clay, was affixed to the stone (i.e., the stone door) and the tomb wall. Therefore, if anyone would have tried to remove the stone from the opening of the tomb, they would have broken the seal and thus incurred the death penalty.

Cephas (i.e., Peter), **then by the twelve; after that, He was seen by over five hundred brethren at once; most of whom remain to this present** *day*, **but some have fallen asleep**" (see 1 Corinthians 15:1-6).

Shortly before Jesus physically ascended into heaven He came to His disciples and said to them, **"All power has been given unto Me in heaven and in earth.**" Then He commanded them, **"Go and make disciples of all nations, baptizing them in the name of the Father, and of the Son, and of the Holy Spirit: teaching them to observe all things, whatsoever I have commanded you"** (see Matthew 28:18-20). And beginning with Jerusalem, the early Christians took the message of Christ into every region of the Middle East, Europe, Africa, and even the Orient. The message of Christ spread so fast that even the enemies of Christ declared, "these men **have turned the world upside down**" (see Acts 17:6).

Now, those are the facts. The British scholar W. H. Griffith Thomas said, "The testimony to the present work of Jesus Christ is no less real today than it has been in the past. In the case of all other great leaders, and great names of the world's history, the inevitable and invariable experience has been that the particular man is first a power, then only a name, and last of all a mere memory. Of Jesus Christ the exact opposite is true. He died on a cross of shame, His name gradually became more and more powerful, and today He is the greatest influence in all the world."[4]

---

[4] W. H. Griffith Thomas, *Christianity is Christ* (London: Church Book Room Press, 1909).

WHO IS THIS MAN?

Now, who is this man, Jesus Christ, whose great influence is still being felt? I think the apostle John may have put it best when he said, **"In the beginning was the Word (Jesus Christ), and the Word was with God, and the Word was God. And the Word was made flesh, and dwelt among us . . ."** (John 1:1 and John 1:14). Jesus Christ was conceived of the Holy Spirit and born of the virgin Mary in Bethlehem over 2,000 years ago. His earthly father was Joseph, a very devout man whose occupation was carpentry.

For most of His life Jesus lived in Nazareth with His parents in virtual obscurity. Then one day, when Jesus was about thirty years old, everything changed. He went to the synagogue on the Sabbath, and while He was there one of the ministers gave Him The Book of Isaiah to read. He opened the book and read these words. **"The Spirit of the Lord *is* upon Me, because He has anointed Me to preach the gospel to the poor; He has sent Me to heal the brokenhearted, to preach deliverance to the captives, and recovering of sight to the blind, to set at liberty them that are bruised, to preach the acceptable year of the Lord."** When He finished reading He closed the book, and gave it back to the minister, and sat down. Then while everyone was still looking at Him He said, "Today this scripture, which you have heard, is fulfilled" (see Luke 4:16-21).

From that moment on, the life Jesus led, the words He spoke, and the miracles He performed all pointed to one fact – that He was more than just a mere man. Think about this for a moment: Mohammed, the founder of the religion of Islam stated, he was a prophet; Confucius, the founder of Confucianism said, he was an ethical teacher; and Siddhartha, the founder of Buddhism declared, he was "the Buddha", which means the enlightened one; but Jesus claimed to be God! He said, **"I and**

My **Father are one"** (John 10:30). He said, **"I am Alpha and Omega, the Beginning and the Ending . . . the Almighty"** (see Revelation 1:8)! Now, when Jesus made these statements He was proclaiming, "I have the same nature, essence, power, and glory as the Father." Thus Jesus Christ claims "absolute deity," "absolute equality" with the Father. Jesus Christ claims to be God!

It is also important to realize that the people around Him: His disciples, and even His enemies, the Jewish leaders knew exactly what He meant. They all recognized that He was making Himself out to be God. No other inference could be drawn. And mark it well, Jesus did not accuse them of misconstruing what He said, or misinterpreting what He meant. Consequently, anyone who simply says that Jesus was a good moral teacher, religious leader, or great prophet, and nothing more, doesn't understand the ramifications of Jesus' words: because a good moral teacher, religious leader, or great prophet would never claim to be God. Therefore, Jesus Christ was either a liar, or He was insane, or, He is God.

But Jesus not only claimed to be God, He proved it, by demonstrating His miraculous power. Jesus gave sight to the blind, healed the deaf, and cleansed lepers. Jesus even delivered those who were demon-possessed! After the apostle John wrote that Jesus walked on water, fed the five thousand, and raised Lazarus from the grave, he made this statement. **"There are also many other things which Jesus did . . . But these are written that you might believe that Jesus is the Christ, the Son of God; and that believing** you **might have life through His name"** (see John 21:25 and John 20:31).

8

WHY DID HE COME?

Now, if Jesus is in fact God: if He truly is the Christ, the Son of God, why did He come to earth? Well, to put it simply, He came to die for our sins. This brings me to point number two: in order to become a Christian, a person must understand why Jesus came to earth. Jesus said, "**the Son of Man did not come to be served, but to serve, and to give His life a ransom for many**" (see Mark 10:45). He also said, "**the Son of Man shall be betrayed** into the hands of **the chief priests, and the scribes, and they shall condemn Him to death**, and they **shall deliver Him to the Gentiles: to mock, and to scourge, and to crucify *Him*; and** on **the third day He shall rise again**" (see Matthew 20:18-19).

So Jesus came in order to die. By the way, can you imagine anyone predicting that in a few weeks they're going to die, and then, come back to life again in three days? I'm sure that if anyone came to you and told you that, you'd think they were crazy. And yet, this is exactly what Jesus did.

But, you ask, "Why did He have to die?" Because that was the only way He could pay for our sins. The Scriptures tell us, "**without** the **shedding of blood** there **is no remission** (or forgiveness) of sins . . ." (see Hebrews 9:22). That's the reason why people regularly brought animals to the priest to be sacrificed during the Old Testament. The priest would kill the animal and then, sprinkle its blood on the altar, as a temporary covering for that person's sins. Now, the animal had to be perfectly healthy in order for the person's sins to be transferred to it. If the animal had a disease it could not be used. If it had any broken bones it could not be used. If the animal even had a spot, or a blemish on it, it could not be used. It had to be perfect! This was "a type," a picture of what would occur when God's one unique lamb would be sacrificed. The only difference being, Jesus' blood would not just cover a person's sins temporarily, His blood would take them away forever.

But before Jesus could die for our sins, He had to live an absolutely holy, righteous, sinless life. If Jesus would have committed one sin, just one, He wouldn't have been fit to die for our sins. But thanks be to God, Jesus never sinned. Never! He never lied, never got drunk, never stole, and never lusted after a woman. He never gossiped, or worried, or committed fornication, or coveted anything! Jesus never had a sinful thought and He never committed a sinful act in His entire life. He never sinned!

THE CRUCIFIXION OF JESUS

Let's look briefly at the crucifixion of Jesus Christ. The apostle Matthew wrote, "the soldiers **crucified Him, and parted His garments, casting lots: that it might be fulfilled which was spoken by the prophet, 'They parted My garments among them, and upon My vesture they did cast lots.' And sitting down they watched Him there; and set up over His head His accusation, written** (in Greek, and Latin, and Hebrew): **THIS IS JESUS, THE KING OF THE JEWS. And there were two thieves crucified with Him, one on the right, and another on the left. And they that passed by reviled Him, wagging their heads, and saying, '. . . save Yourself ! If You are the Son of God, come down from the cross.'"**

But He couldn't come down. If Jesus would have come down from the cross, we would have all been doomed to spend eternity in hell, because we can't pay for our own sins!

The people said, **"He saved others; Himself He cannot save. If He** really is **the King of Israel, let Him come down from the cross now, and we will believe Him."**

Sure, sure you will. . . .

Now from noon until 3 o'clock there was **darkness over all the land.** And at about 3 o'clock **Jesus cried with a loud voice, saying, "Eli, Eli, lama sabachthani?" That is to say, "My God, My God, why hast Thou forsaken Me?"** (see Matthew 27:35-46)

Now why did Jesus say that? I'm sure that when the people heard Him say that some of them must have thought, "Aaah, just another false Messiah."

Why did Jesus say, **"My God, My God, why hast Thou forsaken Me?"** Because at that moment Jesus was experiencing the torment of hell for every man, woman, boy and girl. During those three hours of darkness God, the Father, placed all the sins of the world on Jesus! And when He did, He had to turn His back on His Son. For the first time in all of eternity, fellowship with God and His Son was broken: because God cannot remain where unforgiven sin resides. . . . God hates sin! None of us here can even begin to grasp just how much God hates sin! God hates sin so much, that He forsook His only Son!

Someone once said, "Since Jesus Christ is the only person who has ever lived an absolutely holy, righteous, sinless life, He is the only person who could have given His life to pay for our sins. You see, we cannot pay for our sins, because we are not holy. We are sinful. So Jesus Christ came to earth to live a holy life, and sacrifice Himself for us. He came to die in our place, to pay the penalty for our sins. And to demonstrate that

11

God accepted His death as payment for our sins, He raised Him up from the dead."

SIN MUST BE PAID FOR

All religions teach that sin must be paid for. However only one, Christianity, provides an adequate solution to that dilemma. All other religions teach that a man must earn his own salvation – usually through one of three methods: 1) through doing good works such as obeying the laws of Moses, feeding the poor, loving your neighbor, and caring for widows; 2) through rigid self-denial such as living in extreme poverty, refusing to kill any living thing (including insects), even denying one's self sexual pleasure, and avoiding all worldly attachments; or, 3) through performing religious duties such as worshiping a god, participating in a pilgrimage, meditating, fasting, and praying five times a day.

Of course, the only problem with each of these three methods is, there is no way a person can know, before he dies, if he's done enough to earn his salvation. Thus, at the moment of death, he doesn't know where he will spend eternity. But even though he doesn't know, the Bible clearly states where he will go. You see the Bible says you were born in sin (see John 9:34). The Bible says you can't perform enough good works to earn your salvation because from God's perspective, all of your good works *are* **as filthy rags** (see Isaiah 64:6). The Bible says God hates sin. He hates sin so much, that if you commit just one sin, JUST ONE, you will go to hell. Unless you receive Jesus Christ (see James 2:10-11).

No one can be saved apart from the substitutionary death of Jesus Christ. Don't you see, either you will pay for your sins or Jesus will. Jesus is the only substitute that God has provided for us. By dying on the cross for our sins, Jesus willingly took upon Himself the punishment that each one of us deserves. Therefore, when a person receives Jesus Christ a great exchange takes place. Jesus takes all of our sins, and we receive all of His righteousness! Consequently, when a Christian dies, he will spend eternity in heaven. Why? Because Jesus has paid for all of his sins.

Men and women, make no mistake about it, if you do not receive Jesus Christ as your personal Savior before you die, you will spend all of eternity paying for your sins in the lake of fire. This is what makes Christianity different from all other religions. It offers another method of salvation, which in reality is THE ONLY WAY A PERSON CAN BE SAVED! Let's face it, you can't earn your own salvation. There's no way! There's no way you can do enough, meditate enough, give enough, pray enough, fast enough, or be good enough. Because there's no way you can be holy enough! Therefore, if a person wants to be saved and go to heaven, he or she must receive Jesus Christ. That's why Jesus said, "**I am the way, the truth, and the life: no man comes unto the Father, but by Me**" (John 14:6).

In the spring of 1994 I took a vacation and went to St. Louis, Mo. During my stay I visited a church there and heard the pastor tell the following story during his evening message.

One of the members of his church, named Jeff, went to the park about a week ago. While he was there he met this guy named Mark and shared the gospel with him. Mark had on these reflective glasses and a Bulls T-shirt. He was about 20, and he worked at Six Flags. When Jeff made the transition and turned the conversation to Jesus Christ, Mark started acting really pompous. His attitude was, "You're going to talk to me about religion? Sure, okay." It turned out Mark was your typical "moralist." He believed in obeying the Ten Commandments and doing good deeds. He really felt he was a good person. After all, he wasn't into drugs, or sleeping around. He believed in God! Mark even told Jeff about the time he totaled his truck in a wreck: he walked away with only a few cuts and bruises. He really felt God was with him that day. Then Jeff asked Mark what he thought his chances of getting to heaven were? He felt they were pretty good. Then Jeff asked, "Have you ever sinned?" Mark looked at him for a moment. Then reluctantly said, "Yes." Well to make a long story short, Mark began to see that living a good moral life just wasn't going to be enough to get him into heaven. He needed to receive Jesus, because He was the only one who could pay for his sins. Then Jeff asked him, "Would you like to pray right now, and ask Christ to come into your life?" Mark said, "Yeah, I really would." So he bowed his head, right there in the park, and asked Christ to come into his life, and be his Savior.

THE ROLE OF EMOTIONS

Third, in addition to knowing who Jesus is and why He came, a person must also understand the role, or place of emotions, as it relates to becoming a Christian. An emotion could be defined as a state of feeling, or conscious mental reaction (such as loneliness or confidence), that is subjectively experienced . . .[5]

Everyone experiences emotions. People by nature are emotional creatures. Almost everything a person does causes some kind of emotional response. The way we communicate, the things we buy, the music we listen to, even the food we eat causes some type of emotion. And different people have

[5] Used by permission. From *Merriam-Webster's Collegiate Dictionary, 11th Edition* 2016 by Merriam-Webster, Inc. (www.Merriam-Webster.com).

different emotional responses. Two people may be viewing the same sporting event, but if one is extroverted and highly emotional, and the other is introverted and deeply introspective, they may respond differently. Especially if the team they're rooting for scores at a critical point in the game. One may be jumping up and down cheering ecstatically, and the other may be standing in awe, contemplating the greatness of the play.

TWO DIFFERENT RESPONSES

For many years these differing kinds of emotional responses have caused a great deal of confusion, as it relates to a person becoming a Christian. The Philippian jailer, for example, had an unusually dramatic experience the day he received Christ. The apostle Paul and his partner Silas were thrown in jail illegally during one of their missionary journeys, and this guard was suppose to keep an eye on them, as well as all the other prisoners.

Now all the prisoners were chained in their cells, and all the cells were locked, so the guard decided to take a nap. But at about midnight Paul and Silas began praying and singing hymns to God, and all the other prisoners were listening to them. Then suddenly, there was a great earthquake. And immediately all the doors were opened, and everyone's chains fell off.

And when the guard woke up he thought all the prisoner's had escaped. So he drew out his sword, in order to kill himself. But Paul cried out, saying, "**Do not harm yourself, for we are all here!**" Then the guard, trembling, came to Paul and Silas, and he fell down before them and said, "**Sirs, what must I do to be saved?**" And they said to him, "**Believe on the Lord Jesus Christ and you shall be saved . . .**" So the guard received Christ (see Acts 16:16-34).

Now, when he received Christ the Scriptures say he rejoiced. He rejoiced! That was his emotional response. Now Scripture doesn't clarify and tell us specifically what he did; so we don't know whether he jumped up and down praising God, or cried for joy, or what. All we know is that he was visibly happy. He rejoiced!

Now, while Paul and Silas were on this same missionary journey, they also witnessed to a group of women. One of the women was named Lydia. She was a business woman from Thyatira. As Lydia listened to them, God opened up her heart; and she gave heed to what Paul was saying, and she received Christ (see Acts 16:11-15).

Now when she received Christ nothing extraordinary happened. Well, I shouldn't say that. I mean when God opens up a person's heart to receive Christ that's nothing short of extraordinary. But what I'm saying is, there was no visible display of emotion. Now I know this woman had to be just as happy as that guard was. Yet, she seemingly had no emotional response at all.

EMOTIONS CAN DECEIVE

You know, I'm sure there are many people, who, if asked would say, "When I received Jesus Christ I really didn't have a dramatic emotional experience." Yet most of the time, people hear about those Christians who have had a dramatic conversion experience . . . how that Christ has healed them, or cured them of alcoholism, or straightened out some other distressing problem in their life. Now the fact that their lives were changed indeed validates their claims. But because of this disparity, there are people today who actually believe they will have a dramatic emotional experience when they become a Christian.

However this is not true, or should I say this is not necessarily true. You see, whether you have an emotional experience or not makes no difference at all. Your emotions have nothing to do with you becoming a Christian. The Bible says we are saved by faith (see Ephesians 2:8), not by faith that is accompanied by an emotional experience. The Bible also says, "**the just shall live by faith**" (Hebrews 10:38). Therefore, "**without faith *it is* impossible to please *Him***" (Hebrews 11:6). Did you know that the very act of seeking an emotional experience is the exact opposite of what God wants you to do? God wants you to place your faith (or trust) in Him, and in His Word, rather than in some emotional experience.

Now, having said that, let me say this. There is a place for emotions in the Christian life. In my own life I've experienced times of great rejoicing, and moments of shear delight! (I've also experienced deep sorrow, and intense frustration.) But the key is this. I don't seek emotional experiences. Now, when they happen, that's great. I mean when God blesses me or does something special in my life, believe me, I rejoice! I get happy. I get excited. I don't bury my emotions deep down inside or act somber. My feelings show through! But, I don't attempt to relive or revive experiences from the past. I don't depend or rely upon my emotions, because they can be very deceiving.

Let me give you an example. Now, suppose you accept the Lord Jesus Christ by faith as your Savior tonight, and the next five days you wake-up feeling great; and then, on the sixth day you wake-up feeling lousy. Does that mean Jesus has left you? That you're no longer a Christian? No! Of course not. You're still a Christian. Why? Because you did not become a Christian by having some great feeling or emotional experience. You became a Christian by placing your faith in Jesus Christ!

But if you don't know this you might wake up one morning and get really depressed, wondering what is going on? And it's at times like these that you must remember, a Christian doesn't live by feelings: by how he or she feels. A Christian lives by faith!

When you become a Christian all your problems don't magically disappear. Believe me, you will still experience days when you have problems. But the difference will be, once you receive Jesus Christ, is that now, you will have the Lord to help you solve your problems!

And that is why it is so important to understand the role, or place of emotions; and how emotions relate to a person becoming a Christian. Because if you do not have some dramatic emotional experience when you receive Jesus Christ as your personal Lord and Savior, your emotions may deceive you into thinking that nothing actually happened. But believe me, the moment you receive Jesus Christ by faith (whether you feel anything or not), you will be saved!

Just listen to what the apostle John said. "**The world was made by Him** (Jesus Christ), **and the world did not know Him.** And **He came unto His own, and His own did not receive Him. . . . But,** to **as many as** do receive **Him, to them He** gives **power to become the sons** and daughters **of God,** *even* **to them that believe on His name**" (see John 1:10-12 and 2 Corinthians 6:16-18). The moment you receive Jesus Christ by faith, you will be saved.

AN ACT OF THE WILL

In order to become a Christian then, you must first, honestly face the claims of Jesus Christ. You must logically consider what Jesus said and did; and believe that He is God. Second, you must realize why Jesus came to earth. He came to live a sinless life, and to die for your sins, in order that you might receive Him as your personal Lord and Savior. Third, you must understand the role, or place of emotions. And finally, in order to become a Christian, you must repent of your sins, and receive Jesus Christ by faith, as an act of your will. Let me say that again. A person must repent of their sins, and, receive Jesus Christ as their personal Lord and Savior, by faith, as an act of their will. You don't become a Christian by being a good person, or by being born into a Christian family. You don't become a Christian by doing good works, or by being baptized, or, by becoming a member of a church. You become a Christian by asking the Lord Jesus Christ to come into your heart, to come into your life.

WE MUST REPENT

In order to become a Christian, a person must repent. In Acts 20:21 the apostle Paul said, "**. . . repentance toward God, and faith toward our Lord Jesus Christ**" are necessary for salvation.

The word "repent" comes from the Greek word "metanoeo." It means "to change one's mind." Thus, the word signifies a change of mind that results in a change of attitude. It is the conscious, deliberate act, of an unsaved person, who freely chooses to turn from sin, to the one true God.

When a person repents, they turn from sin. Now listen, it doesn't mean that they no longer sin. It means they change their mind about sin. They no longer see sin as something that is okay to do. They begin to see sin (maybe for the first time) as being wrong, and immoral. They begin to see sin for what it really is – in all its ugliness. Of course, sometimes, when

19

this happens, it makes a person feel disgusted, and ashamed of themselves, and what they've done.

Why should a person repent? Because from God's perspective, there is no such thing as little sins and big sins. They're all big sins. Thus, if you lived your whole life, and the only thing you ever did wrong was tell one "little" white lie, you would be condemned, and cast into hell. Why? Because telling a lie, even a "little" white one, is a BIG sin!

Therefore, we must repent! We must come to the conclusion that we are no good, because if we were truly good, truly righteous, we wouldn't sin. Thus, when a person "truly repents" do you know what they do? They look at their life, and the sins they've committed. And then they turn to God, and come to Him with an attitude of heart that says, "Oh God, unless You do something, for me, and to me, and in me, I'm going to spend eternity in the lake of fire! Because I have sinned" (Revelation 20:11-15)!

Finally, true repentance includes a desire to change. Remember, the word repent means "a change of mind that results in a change of attitude." When a person repents, what they are saying is, "Oh God, I don't want to live like this anymore. What I want, what I desire, is to live a life that is pleasing to You."

WE ARE SAVED BY FAITH

In Ephesians 2:8-9 the apostle Paul said, **"For by grace ye are saved through faith; and that not of yourselves: *it is* the gift of God: not of works, lest anyone should boast."** These are two of the most important verses in the Bible. Yet, many people really don't understand them. What is Paul saying? Well,

Paul is saying a person is saved by faith, by the grace of God. What is grace? Grace is unmerited favor. In other words, you can't earn it. That's why Paul says, it is **not of yourselves**. God freely chooses to give us grace, simply because He loves us.

Next Paul says, *it is* **the gift of God**. What is? Salvation! Our salvation is a gift! And because it's a gift, you can't work for it; which is why Paul says, it's **not of works**. . . . Did you hear that? Paul said you can't work for your salvation. Nor can you work to keep your salvation. Why? Because God doesn't want anyone on earth, or in heaven, to **boast**. God doesn't want anyone saying, "I saved myself." Because there's no way you can save yourself. You're a sinner! Therefore, salvation is a **gift**.

Do you remember when you were just a little child, and it was your birthday? Do you remember what happened? Well, if you're like most people, you had a birthday party. And on that day, all your best friends brought you presents. Right? Well, when they brought their present − when they stuck out their hands, to give you their present − at that moment, you had the option of doing one of two things. You could have accepted their present, and received it. Or you could have rejected it, and told them to keep it. . . . You had two options: you could have accepted it, or rejected it. But you could not have worked for it! Why? Because it's a gift. You can't work for a gift!

Well, in the same way, salvation is a gift! It's a gift from God. And because it's a gift, YOU CAN'T WORK FOR IT! All you can do is accept it, or reject it. Have you accepted and received God's free gift of salvation? Have you received His Son Jesus Christ into your heart − into your life?

Sometimes when I talk to people who have not received Christ, it becomes obvious that they understand who Jesus is, and why He came. Some even understand the role of emotions.

But the reason why they haven't received Christ yet is because they are reluctant to give their lives to Him. Because they fear He will change their plans, or take all the joy out of life. They see God as some kind of cosmic killjoy, with a baseball bat ready to make their lives miserable. But when you give your life to Christ and commit yourself to Him, you can be absolutely sure that He will not withhold any good thing from you (see Psalm 84:11). Christ Himself assures us: He came in order that we might have an abundant life (see John 10:10).

A FEW REASONS WHY

Many people, such as students, choose not to receive the Lord Jesus because they enjoy getting drunk, or getting high on drugs; they enjoy having sex outside of marriage, and they simply don't want to stop. They can't imagine anything else that could be better. But God says, **"Eye has not seen, nor ear heard, neither have entered into the heart of man, the things which God has prepared for them that love Him"** (1 Corinthians 2:9).

Many years ago, when I was a student at the University of Kansas, I knew a guy who was involved in all of these things. He had all the liquor he could drink, he went to classes high, and he slept with a different girl every week. Man, he really thought he was living. Then one day someone on campus shared Christ with Him. And to everyone's surprise he received Christ. Within a few weeks his lifestyle changed dramatically, and during that semester he became one of the most dynamic Christians on campus. About a year later I got an opportunity to talk to him. During our conversation he spoke of his former life. Do you want to know what he told me? You are not going to believe this, but he told me his life was empty! Empty without Jesus! But now his life was fulfilling! You could see it on his face! God had showed him that what he thought was an exciting life was nothing compared to the abundant life which Jesus offers.

Another reason why people are hesitant to receive Christ is because they are afraid of being a hypocrite. They know their own sins and weaknesses, and fear they will not be able to live up to the standards of the Christian life. But the Bible tells us, in fact reassures us that, "**I can do all things through Christ which strengthens me**" (Philippians 4:13). God never intended us to live the Christian life in our own strength. That's why Christianity is so uniquely different from every other religion. It is not based on human effort. It is not based on will power. It's based on Christ's power. That's why we must ask Christ to come into our life. When we receive Christ, He literally comes inside our body. Then, from within, Christ changes our desires and gives us the power to live the Christian life.

Many successful business men and women have also refused to receive Jesus Christ, because they think they'll have to sell all their possessions, and give the proceeds to the poor. But God doesn't usually lead a person to do that. Oh, every now and then He does, but usually He doesn't, because it's not sinful to be wealthy. It's not a sin to own material things. But even if God did lead you to sell most of what you own, would that really be so bad? I mean in the final analysis, "**what shall it profit a man, if he shall gain the whole world, and lose his own soul**" (Mark 8:36)? Or to put it another way, money can buy a lot of things, but money still can't buy love, joy, peace, contentment, or eternal life.

One business woman shared, "I had a very good home life, and a better than average education. Shortly after I graduated from college I opened up my own interior design firm and became financially secure rather early in life. I devoted myself entirely to my work. But after a few years I became disillusioned with the clients, deadlines, contractors, etc. I was also very lonely. I had become a workaholic.

"Then, he walked into my life. The man of my dreams, or so I thought. I fell in love and about a year later we got married. I thought, now finally, my life is complete: I'm my own boss, I'm wealthy, and I'm in love! And then the bottom dropped out. While I was pregnant with our second child, my husband left me for another woman! I was so devastated. I felt like someone had sawed me in two!

"Then one Saturday afternoon, when I was at home feeling real depressed, a young woman came to my house and shared the gospel with me. All my life I had thought I didn't need God. But now, for the first time, I realized I did. I really did. So I bowed my head and asked Jesus Christ to come into my life, and save me. Ever since that day my life has taken on new meaning. Now my life really is complete."

There are others who have not received Christ yet because they feel like they have to clean up their life first. They think they have to stop doing this, and quit doing that; get rid of this, and give up that, before they can come to God. However, Scripture tells us that there is no way we can make ourselves right before God. Isaiah 64:6 says, **"But we are all as an unclean *thing*, and all our righteousnesses *are* as filthy rags . . ."** You see, we must come to God just as we are, because He is the only one who can clean us up. He says, **"Come now, and let us reason together . . . though your sins be as scarlet, they shall be as white as snow"** (Isaiah 1:18).

Still others have not asked Christ to come into their lives because they feel they have committed too many sins, or some sin that is so horrible that God would never forgive them. But the Bible says, **"For the Son of Man** has **come to seek and to save that which was lost"** (see Luke 19:10). Notice, Jesus doesn't put any stipulations on who can or cannot be saved. He says He came to seek and to save anyone, and everyone, who is lost.

The apostle Paul is the classic example. Here is a man who truly served God, a man whom we admire, whom we attempt to emulate. And yet we sometimes forget, that before he was saved, Paul persecuted Christians. He vehemently hated believers. So much so that he blasphemed God. He cursed Jesus, and probably thought He was an agent of Satan. He ridiculed Christians. He beat them. He even attempted to put all Christians, both men and women in prison. He confiscated their property: their homes, their clothing, their money. God only knows what he did to their kids.

But one day, while Paul was traveling on the road to Damascus, the Lord Jesus appeared to him, and saved him. And a few weeks later Paul began preaching the gospel of Christ in the synagogues.

But lest anyone forget what kind of person he really was, Paul says, "I was the worst sinner who ever lived." Now when Paul says, "He was the chiefest of sinners," he is not simply using oratorical rhetoric. He is not exaggerating. He is telling the truth.

Paul was a blasphemer and a persecutor of the church, and yet Jesus saved him (see 1 Timothy 1:13-15). But that's an ancient example. Let me give you a more recent one.

On April 16th Don was put in prison for robbing a gas station and shooting the attendant. About a year after he was placed behind bars, a young man from one of the churches in town, invited him to attend the prison's worship service. Don recalls, "I was playing checkers with another inmate at the time, so I told him I don't believe in that stuff; you're wasting your time. Go brainwash, ah save, somebody else!

"For the next two years different people invited me to come to the service. Even some of the fellahs invited me to come, but I always refused. Actually, I felt like God would never forgive me, because I killed a man in cold blood.

"Then on Easter Sunday I was invited again to come. And I decided, what the λ ξ ϑ𝓛 ζ, I got nothin' better to do. As the preacher spoke about Jesus' death and resurrection, and how He came to save us, no matter what we'd done, I was moved. I began to think, maybe God could forgive me. I thought about what that preacher said all week. And the more I thought about it the more I believed it. So the very next Sunday, when the invitation was given, I got up and went down to talk to that preacher. I told him I wanted to be saved! So he asked me, 'Do you believe in God?' I said, 'Yes.' Then he asked me, 'Have you repented of your sins?' Again, I said, 'Yes.' Finally he asked me, 'Do you believe that Jesus died for your sins and rose again?' I told him, 'YES!' So the preacher invited me to bow my head and pray, and ask the Lord Jesus Christ to come into my heart. . . . Well, ever since that day, I've never doubted God's forgiveness, or His love for me. It's just like the Bible says, 'Jesus really did come to save everyone.'"

Now, if Jesus can save a man who persecuted Christians, and, a murderer, He can save you. If Jesus can save drunks, and gamblers, and homosexuals, He can save you. If Jesus can save adulterers, gossips, liars, drug addicts, prostitutes, and thieves, He can save you. Jesus came to seek and to save you. Yes, even you.

RECEIVE JESUS CHRIST BY FAITH

Does everything that I have said make sense to you? Have you ever personally asked Jesus Christ to come into your life and be your Lord and Savior? Are you sure you're saved? If you were to die, right now, are you sure you would spend eternity with God in heaven? If you cannot answer "yes" to these questions, I urge you to receive Jesus Christ by faith today.

What does it mean to receive Christ by faith? It means that we receive Him, believing that He will save us. John 3:16 says, **"For God so loved the world, that He gave His only begotten Son, that whosoever believes in Him should not perish, but have everlasting life."** Therefore, to receive Christ means, that we are no longer trusting in our own ability to keep the Ten Commandments, or do good works, or get baptized, to be saved. It means that we are trusting and relying on Christ, and Him alone, to save us. . . . It also means that when we ask Him to come into our heart and life, we must believe that He will really come in, and dwell (or live) within us. In Revelation 3:20 Jesus says, **"Behold, I stand at the door, and knock: if anyone** will **hear My voice, and open the door, I will come in to him, and will sup** (i.e., dine and fellowship) **with him, and he with Me."**

RECEIVE JESUS CHRIST NOW

You can receive the Lord Jesus Christ right now by praying the following prayer below. Now, I'm sure some of you are probably saying, "That's too easy. There must be something else I have to do?" Is it really "easy?" Remember, by praying, you are giving your life to Christ. You are asking Him, to take control of your life! But also remember, if you pray in faith, believing that Jesus will come into your life – you will become a Christian, and you will spend eternity with God in heaven.

So come on, I urge you. Receive Jesus Christ now!

Pray the following prayer:

"Lord Jesus, I need you. I know that I have sinned. I do believe that the Father sent You to shed Your blood for me, to die on the cross in my place, and to pay the penalty for all my sins. So right now, I repent of my sins, and ask You to forgive my sins. And I open the door of my heart, and my life, and receive you as my Lord and Savior. Thank you for forgiving my sins and for coming into my life. And thank you for giving me eternal life. Now take my life and direct me, and make me the type of person You want me to be. In Jesus' name I pray. Amen."

Did you pray and ask the Lord Jesus to come into your life by faith? If you did, let me be the first to welcome you into the Family of God. You can be sure now that Jesus lives inside of you, and, that you have eternal life. For the Holy Bible says, **"And this is the record, that God has given to us eternal life, and this life is in His Son. He that has the Son has life;** *and* **he that does not have the Son of God does not have life. These things I have written unto you that believe on the name of the Son of God, in order that you may know that you have eternal life . . ."** (see 1 John 5:11-13).

THINGS TO REMEMBER AND DO

But again, the question may arise, "What if I don't feel any different?" Don't worry about your feelings. Remember, you are saved because you asked the Lord Jesus to come into your life by faith, not because you feel any different.

Always remember this day too, because this is your spiritual birthday. Never forget that on this day you became a Christian. And remember also to thank God often, because Jesus now lives inside of you, and He has given you eternal life.

Finally, let me encourage you to attend a good Bible-believing church on a regular basis. The Scriptures say, do not forsake **"the assembling of ourselves together, as the manner of some** *is* **. . ."** (Hebrews 10:25). You see, it is God's desire that we become active members of a local church, because He knows we will be taught, encouraged, comforted, and strengthened there.

If you do not belong to a church, I would suggest that you pray first and ask God to lead and direct you. Then go and visit several churches in the area where you live. When you find a church where God is worshipped, the Bible is taught, and the Lord Jesus is preached as man's only means of salvation, go and talk to the Pastor. And when the invitation is given at the end of the service, tell him that you have received Jesus Christ as your personal Lord and Savior, and, that you want to become a member of the church.

The Issue of Eternal Security (Part One)

CHAPTER TWO

When I was a young Christian, just beginning to grow spiritually, a good Christian friend of mine came over to visit me. During our conversation we talked about several things: how I was doing; whether or not we thought the Royals would beat the Yankees in the playoffs; and how things were going on his job. But the one thing that sticks out in my mind, even to this day, is that he asked me a question I had never really thought about before. And that question was, "Michael, are you sure you have eternal life?" No one had ever asked me that question before.

I thought to myself, "Well, I know I'm a Christian, I attend church regularly, I give money to the church, I try to live right, and I witness to people." So I looked at my friend and I said, "I guess so." He said, "You guess so! Michael don't you know?" I looked at him and said, "What do you mean?" He said, "Are you sure? Absolutely, positively, one hundred percent sure, that when you die you will spend eternity in heaven with God?" I had to admit, I wasn't. At least, not one hundred percent sure. Well, he got my Bible and read to me the following passage:

> **"And this is the record, that God has given to us eternal life, and this life is in His Son. He that has the Son has life; *and* he that does not have the Son of God does not have life. These things I have written unto you that believe on the name of the Son of God; in order that** you **may know that** you **have eternal life . . ."** (see 1 John 5:11-13)

Then he explained to me that God had the apostle John write this passage to assure us, Christians, of the fact that we have eternal life. He explained, verse 12 means that if a person has received Jesus Christ as their personal Lord and Savior they can be absolutely sure they have eternal life. Why? Because the verse says, **"he that has the Son has life."** In other words, a person who has received Christ ALREADY HAS ETERNAL LIFE. Then in verse 13 the apostle says, I wrote this **"that** you **may KNOW that** you **have eternal life."** Notice, John didn't write that you might hope to have eternal life, or wonder about whether or not you have eternal life. He said, **"These things I have written unto you that believe on the name of the Son of God; in order that** YOU **MAY KNOW that** you **have eternal life."**

After my friend explained the passage, he turned to me and said, "Michael, based on these verses God says you can know beyond any shadow of a doubt that you have eternal life, because you have received the Lord Jesus Christ." Well, I want you to know that night I went to bed with an assurance I'd never had before; the assurance that I have eternal life: the assurance that when I died I would spend eternity in heaven with God.

Then, about two years later, I met for the first time a Christian who told me he didn't believe a person could ever be absolutely sure about their eternal destiny. In fact, he told me the ministers at his church teach that a Christian can never be certain he has eternal life, because there is always the possibility he might lose his salvation.

YOU MUST DECIDE

Well to put it bluntly, it was on that day that I learned the issue of "eternal security" is one of the most controversial issues in all of Christendom. I mean I had never heard anyone say it was possible for a Christian to lose his salvation before. So do you know what I did? I asked my Bible study leader, "Who was right? My friend, or this other Christian?" Guess what he did?

He gave me a list of verses stating both sides of the issue, a book on eternal security, and a cassette tape entitled, "Can A Person Be Sure?" Then he told me, "You must decide for yourself." It's not that he didn't know who was right. He just wanted me to decide for myself. So for the next year I studied both sides of this issue. I prayed and asked God to show me the truth. I examined both points of view in as unbiased a manner as possible, and I came to the conclusion that a Christian CAN BE SURE he has eternal life. What I want to do in this lesson is share with you why I came to that conclusion.

THIS IS THE STARTING POINT

But before we get into this lesson let me make a couple more introductory comments. You may be wondering, since this is such a controversial issue, and since there are Christians who in fact do not believe a Christian can be sure he has eternal life, why do we need to study this? Why can't we just skip this lesson and go on to the next one? Because this is the starting point! This is the starting point of spiritual maturity! And, this is the starting point of Christian service! You see, you cannot grow into full and complete maturity, as a Christian, until you settle this issue in your life. Indeed, until this issue is settled your spiritual growth will be stunted. Your spiritual growth will be impeded, both intellectually and emotionally, causing you to grow abnormally: causing you to serve God out of fear instead of love.

WHO AM I TALKING ABOUT

Now, as we ponder this issue of whether or not a person can be sure he or she has eternal life, you must understand that I am talking about a "Christian." In other words, a person who has received Jesus Christ as their personal Lord and Savior; a person who has truly been born again by placing their faith in Jesus of Nazareth, the Son of God; a person who has as an act of their will asked the Lord Jesus Christ to come into their heart and life by faith.

God never promises eternal life to a person who does religious things, like joining a church, or getting baptized, or doing good works, or giving money, or spending time in prayer, or keeping the Ten Commandments, or whatever. God only promises eternal life to a Christian: a person who has received Jesus Christ by faith.

You must also understand, and this is very important – you must understand that I am talking about Christians who live in "this age" of the New Testament. I am not talking about believers who lived during the Old Testament times. Nor am I talking about people who will live during the Tribulation Period or for that matter people who will live during the Millennial Kingdom Age when Christ will rule for a thousand years. The Bible never promises these people the assurance of eternal life; only Christians who live in the New Testament Church Age.

THE DISPENSATIONS OF SCRIPTURE

This brings me to the last piece of introductory information. We need to have a general understanding of the dispensations of Scripture. Now, don't go to sleep on me. This will become extremely important when we start looking at those controversial verses. Colossians 1:25-27 says, **"whereof I am made a minister, according to the dispensation of God which is given to me for you, to fulfill the word of God;** *even* **the mystery which has been hid from ages and from generations, but now is made manifest to His saints: to whom God would make known what** *is* **the riches of the glory of this mystery among the Gentiles; which is Christ in you, the hope of glory."**

There's our word – dispensation. This word comes from the Greek word "oikonomia." When you study the history of this word you'll discovery "oikonomia" is a combination of two Greek words: "oikos" which means house, and "nomus" which means law. Thus "oikonomia" means "the law of the house." It primarily refers to household administration: the rules and regulations by which a household is operated; the way in which the master of the house manages and governs his household.

This is very important to understand and grasp, because many people believe the Greek word "oikonomia" means "a period of time." Therefore, they define a "dispensation" as "a period of time." But that is a mistaken, inaccurate meaning.

Well if a dispensation is not a period of time, what is a dispensation? Well, Biblically speaking, a "dispensation" is "a distinct manner, or method, which the Lord uses, to manage and govern the world (which is His household), as He progressively works out His plan of redemption." For lack of a better phrase, it is "a distinct period of human history" during which:

1. God gives mankind some specific revelation. God tells man do this, and you shall live and be blessed, and, you shall be saved.

2. Mankind is then tested with respect to his obedience concerning that revelation.

3. Mankind fails that test, which ultimately brings about God's condemnation of mankind and judgment. Which then causes (or constrains) God to move to the next phase of His plan to redeem humanity, and, bring glory to Himself.

Notice, I said, "Which then causes God to move to the next phase of His plan to redeem (i.e., save) humanity, and, bring glory to Himself!" In each dispensation God gives "specific revelation" concerning how people are to be saved during that specific period of human history. Did you know that people in the Old Testament were not saved like you and me today?

Well, what are these dispensations? And how many dispensations are there in the Bible?[1] The dispensations are as follows:

---

[1] Dispensations in Scripture began to be recognized, and taught, as early as the 2nd century. Back then, several early Church leaders taught that there were four distinct dispensations. Then, in the 17th century, because of the advancements that had been made in the study of the Scriptures, many ministers and theologians began to teach that there were at least 5, or maybe

1. The Dispensation of Innocence (the fall).

2. The Dispensation of Conscience (one offering).

3. The Dispensation of Corruption (the flood).

4. The Dispensation of Human Government (the tower of Babel).

5. The Dispensation of the Promise (several offerings).

6. The Dispensation of the Law (daily offerings).

7. The Dispensation of Grace: the church age (Ephesians 3:2). This is the dispensation (period of human history) that we are living in. Christ in you, the hope of glory (Colossians 1:25-27).

8. The Dispensation of Tribulation (the time of Jacob's trouble).

9. The Dispensation of the Kingdom (the millennial kingdom age).

10. The Dispensation of the Fullness of Times.

Now, why did I go through this? Why did I go through the dispensations with you? Because I want you to be aware of the

---

6 dispensations. Today, many Christians teach that there are 7 or 8 distinct dispensations: mainly because the church now has a better understanding of prophecy, since Israel has gone back to her land. But I have chosen to view dispensations differently. Because in my own personal study, I have seen how God has chosen to save people during different periods of human history! Therefore, I have come to the conclusion that there are 10 distinct dispensations.

fact that in each dispensation God has chosen to save people in a specific (i.e., different) way.

And this is extremely important to understand, because the reason why some Ministers teach that Christians can lose their salvation is because they don't understand that we don't have to keep the law, like they did in the Old Testament. Nor do we have to endure to the end, as the people in the Tribulation will have to. All we have to do TODAY is receive the Lord Jesus Christ by faith! Consequently, what you're going to see in this study is that people are misinterpreting Scriptures, or people are applying Scriptures to Christians that should only be applied to people in the Old Testament, the Tribulation, or the Millennium.

Therefore, as we ponder this issue of whether or not a person can be sure he has eternal life, you must understand that I am talking about a "Christian" who lives in this "New Testament Church Age."

By the way, it is important to realize that the "New Testament" began when Christ died because the Bible says, in order for a testament to be put in force (in order for the New Testament to begin), there must of necessity "**be the death of the testator**" (see Hebrews 9:15-17). Many people think the New Testament begins at Matthew 1:1. But this is not true. The New Testament begins with the death of Christ which is recorded in Matthew 27:50, Mark 15:37, Luke 23:46, and John 19:30. So, when I speak of Christians who live in "this age," I'm talking about a period of time which began with the death of Christ and which will end with the rapture of the Church; which by the way is recorded in 1 Thessalonians 4:13-17.

TWO CRITICAL QUESTIONS

With this in mind I want you to consider two questions. First, does God provide salvation, or does man do something to obtain salvation? In the final analysis, does God save us, or do we contribute something to what Christ has done to secure our own salvation? This is important, because if God does the saving, He will devise a plan that takes into account every contingency. And then, provide what we need to ensure our salvation. But if we have to do something, there is the possibility that we might make a mistake, or not do enough to fulfill our part of the bargain, and thus forfeit our salvation.

To find the answer to this question we must turn to 1 John 4:14. Listen to the words of the apostle. He says, **"the Father sent** (or provided) **the Son *to be* the Savior of the world."** Who sent the Son? The Father did. How did the Son become the Savior? Well, by dying on the cross in our place He became the all-sufficient, sacrificial Lamb of God, who took our sins away. Did man do anything? No! In fact, Titus 3:5 says, God has saved us (past tense) **"not by works of righteousness which we have done** (Ephesians 2:9 says, "lest anyone should boast"), **but according to His mercy He saved us . . ."** Therefore, **"whosoever shall call upon the name of the Lord shall be** – not might be (there is no doubt about it) – **shall be saved"** (Romans 10:13).

The second question I want you to consider is this. Are the saved promised eternal life, or, a chance to receive eternal life? Let me put it another way. Does God give the believer eternal life, with no strings attached, or does God give eternal life stipulating we have to live right in order to keep it? This is a crucial point, because if there are no strings attached, we do not need to fear what will happen when we die. On the other hand, if we have to continue to live right, we will forever live in fear that one day, we might commit too many sins, or that one sin which would cause us to lose our eternal life.

To answer this question, we turn to the 10th chapter of the Gospel of John. In verse 28 Jesus says, **"I give unto them eternal life . . ."** Not a chance to receive eternal life, but eternal life. Then He says, **"they shall never perish."** What? "They shall NEVER perish!" Notice, Jesus doesn't say, "I will give unto them eternal life if they continue to live right." There is not one stipulation given. Why not? Because when Jesus died on the cross He paid the penalty for ALL our sins: all the sins we've committed in the past, all the sins we will commit today, and all the sins we will ever commit in the future. Acts 13:39 says, **"and by Him all that believe are justified from all things, from which ye could not be justified by the laws of Moses."** There is nothing (no thing) we can do, no sin we can commit, that will ever cause us to lose our eternal life. We can never perish! That's why Jesus says, **"Verily, verily, I say unto you, He that hears My word and believes . . . has everlasting life, and shall not come into condemnation; but has** (already) **past from death to life"** (see John 5:24).

THOSE CONTROVERSIAL PASSAGES

By now you're probably beginning to wonder, if what I'm telling you is really true and there is absolutely no way a "Christian" in "this age" can ever lose his salvation, why is there so much debate over this issue? Well, the fact is, there are a number of verses in the Bible which, at first glance, seem to support the view that a Christian can lose his salvation. Because of this, there are many people who teach that a Christian can be saved today, but lose his salvation tomorrow.

However, if a person takes the time to study these verses very carefully, with an open mind, I honestly believe that they will come to the conclusion that a Christian is eternally secure. The Bible never teaches, NEVER TEACHES, that a Christian can lose his salvation. There is not one verse in the Bible that teaches that. To show you what I mean, I want us to take a look at some of these verses. Now obviously, we don't have time to look at all of them, but I do want to take some time to show you several verses which are commonly used to teach that a Christian can lose his salvation.

The first passage I want us to look at is Matthew 7:21-23, which says, **"Not every one that says unto Me, Lord, Lord, shall enter into the kingdom of heaven; but he that does the will of My Father which is in heaven. Many will say to Me in that day, Lord, Lord, have we not prophesied in Thy name? and in Thy name have cast out demons? and in Thy name done many wonderful works? And then I will profess unto them, I never knew you: depart from Me, ye that work iniquity."**

Many people use this passage to try to teach that if a Christian doesn't do the will of the Father (i.e., doesn't live right, or doesn't obey God), he will not get to heaven. But is that what the passage means? No, not at all. Matthew isn't talking about Christians. He's talking about "people" who say "Lord, Lord." You see, not everyone who professes to be a Christian really is. There are many people today who do wonderful works, who actually think they will go to heaven when they die.

Did you know there are people who spend their whole lives raising money for incurable diseases, who feed the homeless, who use their clairvoyant abilities to help police catch criminals? There are false religious leaders who receive visions, and ministers (who have been deceived) who teach false doctrine. . . . Men and women use white magic to cure sickness, astrology to predict the future, and divining rods to help communities find underground springs. There are social workers who rehabilitate criminals, and athletes who sponsor programs to help under privileged kids. . . . There are untrained physicians (people who have never gone to medical school, who are deceived by demons) who perform surgery and heal people by supernatural means. Jesus says, some will even prophesy in My name and cast out demons. But notice, these people have never truly received Christ, because He says, **"I never knew you."** Now when Jesus says, **"I never knew you,"** He doesn't mean He doesn't know about them. Of course He does! Come on, He's God! He knows all about them! What He means is I never knew you, either as a friend or a follower.

This is very important because in John 10:14 Jesus says, **"I am the good shepherd, and I know My *sheep* . . ."** Jesus says, I know who has truly received Me. In fact, I am intimately acquainted with them. You see, this verse totally refutes the idea that a "Christian" can lose his salvation, because Jesus can never say to the Christian, "I never knew you." Therefore, Matthew 7:21-23 isn't talking about Christians.

All right, let's look at another one. Galatians 5:4 says, **"Christ is become of no effect unto you, whosoever of you are justified by the law; ye are fallen from grace."**

This verse has been used by people since 400 A.D. to try to prove that Christians can lose eternal life. Now how a person could ever come to that conclusion I'll never know. For if you read the Book of Galatians the first thing you'll notice is that the apostle Paul is writing to refute the heresy of the Judaizers (false teachers), who were telling the Galatians they had to be circumcised and keep the law in order to be saved (see Galatians 2:3-5, 3:10, 4:21, 5:12, and 6:12-13). The second thing you will notice is that this is the only letter Paul ever wrote to a church where he doesn't address the people as "saints" or "holy." You see, Paul realizes that many of the people he is writing to are not saved. As a result, you'll find many verses in the Book of Galatians that are written to the lost.

This is the case in chapter five. Paul tells those who haven't received Christ, but who are considering Him, "You can attempt to be justified by getting circumcised and keeping the law, or, you can be justified by placing your faith in Jesus Christ and receiving Him." Beginning with verse 2 he tells them **if ye be circumcised** (i.e., if ye are, or become circumcised) **Christ shall profit you nothing**. Why? Because if you get circumcised you have to do the whole law: you have to obey every Old Testament commandment and fulfill every requirement of the law (see verse 3). So what Paul is dealing with here is two different methods of salvation, two different ways a person can be saved.

When the Old Covenant was established back in Exodus, one of the most important requirements of the law was to be circumcised. Therefore, if you did not get circumcised, you would be cut off from the people of God. Why? Because you would be in violation of God's Covenant. Therefore, if you did not get circumcised, you could not be saved (see Exodus 24:1-12, Genesis 17:1-14, Exodus 12:43-50, and Acts 15:1-35)!

But now, because Jesus has lived a sinless life, and died for our sins, we are no longer obligated to keep all those Old Testament commandments, if – if we receive Jesus Christ as our Lord and Savior by faith. Are you beginning to understand the issue?

Now, I want you to just think about that for a minute. You can be saved by being circumcised and keeping all the Old Testament laws. Do you know how many Old Testament laws there are? Over six hundred! So, in order to be saved, you would have to be circumcised, and, keep the ten commandments, and keep all the Sabbath laws, and keep all the holy day and feast laws, and keep all the cleansing laws, and keep all the food laws, and keep all the sexual laws, and keep all the tithing and monetary and property laws, and, keep all the laws that relate to how you should treat people: your parents, spouses, children, neighbors, servants, etc.

Of course, no mere human can keep all those commandments. That's why God instituted the sacrificial system. But guess what! There are no priests performing animal sacrifices in Jerusalem today! Now true enough, when Paul wrote this in 50 A.D. they were still performing animal sacrifices. But animal sacrifices were eliminated in 70 A.D. So guess what! After 70 A.D., you couldn't keep the Old Testament laws, even if you wanted to!

Which brings us, believe it or not, right back where we started from. Because Paul said in Galatians 3:24, "that **the law was our schoolmaster** (or teacher) *to bring us* **unto Christ, that we might be justified by faith.**" The purpose of the law was to teach people that they couldn't keep it. No man or woman can keep the whole law! So Paul says, you can "attempt" to be justified by the law (you won't be, but you can "attempt" to be), or, you can be justified by grace through faith in Jesus Christ!

Now do you understand what Paul is really dealing with here? Paul is talking about two different methods of salvation. You can either be saved by obeying the law, or, you can be saved by grace through faith (Ephesians 2:8-9). Therefore, verse 4, whoever attempts to be justified by the law falls (or turns away) from the method of salvation by grace. You see, this passage has nothing to do with a Christian losing eternal life; it's talking about two different methods of salvation.

Let me say one more thing before we move on. Even though these verses were written to non-Christians, they can be applied to Christians. For Paul tells the Christians in Galatians 5:1 **"Stand fast therefore in the liberty wherewith Christ has made us free, and do not be entangled again with the yoke of bondage."** Paul says to the Christian, "Now that you have been saved by grace, don't go back to living under the law, thinking this will help ensure your salvation."

If a Christian goes back to living by the law after he has been saved by grace, he, "in a sense," falls from grace too! You see, grace is not only the unmerited favor of God bestowed upon mankind, it is a realm or sphere in which the Christian is supposed to live. When we live in this realm, we avail ourselves to God's storehouse of innumerable gifts and blessings (e.g., strength, food, comfort, peace, shelter, patience, courage, support and many other provisions) that are given to us to sustain us and meet our every need (see 2 Corinthians 9:8 and 12:9). But if we go back to living under the law, we fall (or turn away) from the realm of grace, and close (or at the very least block) the door to God's storehouse of blessings (see Galatians 2:21).

Now turn to Hebrews 6:4-6. Before we begin I should warn you, this is one of the most debated passages in all the Bible. It reads, **"For *it is* impossible for those who were once enlightened, and have tasted of the heavenly gift, and were made partakers of the Holy Spirit, and have tasted the good word of God, and the powers of the world to come, if they shall fall away, to renew them again unto repentance; seeing they crucify to themselves the Son of God afresh, and put *Him* to an open shame."** Generally speaking, when you narrow down all the various views and explanations concerning these verses, you'll find that most Christians believe one of the following three interpretations.

First, some Christians believe the people spoken of in these verses are not really Christians. They argue that these people made some sort of outward profession of faith without really asking Christ to come into their lives; that they simply became members of a local church without actually receiving Christ. Now, I must be honest with you. I personally find this view very hard to believe. In the first place the Bible never exhorts unbelievers to go on to "perfection," which means completeness or maturity here (see Hebrews 5:11-6:3). On top of that, verse 4 tells us they were made "PARTAKERS" of the Holy Spirit.

Now, those who teach that these people were not really saved will explain that "partakers" means that they agreed with, or went along with the Holy Spirit . . . they associated with the Holy Spirit, but never received Him. However, this is not true. The word "partaker" means to take, or have a share in. These people "took" or "received" into their body the Holy Spirit. They "possessed" the Spirit (compare this verse with 2 Peter 1:4). Of course, no one can possess, or be endowed with the Holy Spirit unless they are a Christian.

The second interpretation which is used to explain these verses is that these are Christians who lost their salvation. Those who believe this view say that if a Christian falls away (stops living right and backslides) they will lose their salvation. What is strange about this view is that verse 4 says, ". . . it is 'impossible' to renew them." In other words, if a Christian ever fell away and lost his salvation, it would be **impossible** for him to get saved again. Yet most of the people who hold this view teach that a person can get saved over and over and over again. In fact, they constantly plead with backsliders to come back to the Lord: to get right and be saved all over again.

The second point of contention with this view is that these verses really aren't talking about salvation. They're talking about "repentance." Notice, the verse doesn't say it's impossible to renew them to salvation. It says it's impossible to renew them to "**repentance**." What does that mean? Well, that brings me to the third and what I believe is the correct interpretation.

From a historical standpoint, these verses are talking about people, who were Christians, living in the first century; but, who were contemplating going back to the Old Testament Jewish system of sacrifices, because they were being persecuted. In fact, Hebrews 10:32-37 tells us they were under great persecution! From a contemporary (i.e., present day) standpoint, the verses are talking about Christians, who, because of persecution (1 Thessalonians 2:13-3:8); or some tragedy (James 1:2-12); or thorns (Matthew 13:7, 22); or a lack of training (Acts 14:21-23); or continual carnality (1 Corinthians 3:1-3); or willful sin (Hebrews 10:26), or some other reason, "fall away" or "turn away" from the faith.

Now in either case, whether historical or contemporary, when a Christian falls (or turns) away from the faith, he crucifies to himself the Son of God. In other words, even though he didn't literally crucify Christ, he exhibits in his heart and mind the same attitude as those Jews who said, "blessed be the King that comes in the name of the Lord" one day, and "crucify Him" the next. He exhibits the same attitude as Pilate who on the one hand said, "I find no fault in Him," but on the other hand delivered Him up to be crucified. He crucifies to himself Christ! On top of that, the verse also says, "he openly puts Christ to shame!" When he falls away he causes the unsaved to say, "What a crock! Man, I knew when he became a Christian it wouldn't last. I even tried to tell him all that religious mumbo jumbo was worthless. . . . What a waste of time."

Now, because of this, the verse says, "*it is* **impossible to renew them again to repentance**." This phrase can be explained in two ways. And notice, both explanations are applicable. First, sometimes, a Christian who has fallen away (by the grace of God) comes back to once again place their faith in Christ. When this happens, usually, at some point in time the person wishes they could go back and wipe the slate clean: get saved all over again. But you see, they can't. It's impossible to renew them to repentance. They can't go back to the day when they repented of their sins and got saved. They can't get saved again. Why? Because they've already done that! They're already saved! . . . They never lost their salvation! . . . What they may have lost was many, if not most of their rewards. But they never lost their salvation. . . . You see, even though this person may go on to live a committed, fruitful, Christian life, the damage has been done. He has caused sinners to mock Christ and ridicule the cause of Christianity.

The second explanation, and this is what usually happens, is that the Christian who falls away never (sometimes, because God never allows him to) comes back. As a result, he lives the rest of his life "on the shelf" so to speak, because he is no longer useful to Christ. Thus, it is impossible to renew him to repentance because he either won't or can't repent. Now once again, when this Christian dies he won't lose his salvation. What he will lose however, is most, if not all, of his rewards (see 1 Corinthians 3:10-15).

Okay, let's take another passage. In Matthew 8:11-12 Jesus states, **"That many shall come from the east and west, and shall sit down with Abraham, and Isaac, and Jacob, in the kingdom of heaven. But the children of the kingdom shall be cast out into outer darkness: there shall be weeping and gnashing of teeth."**

I can just imagine someone reading that and saying, "See here, this says some children of God shall lose their salvation and go to hell." Does it? Really? . . . Well, before I explain this passage let me remind you of something. Remember at the outset we said that the New Testament doesn't begin until Jesus dies. Well, that little bit of information becomes very important here. You see, in these verses Jesus is talking to people who are living "in" the Old Testament. None of them have been promised the "assurance" of eternal life. Therefore, a person living during this period of time could in fact lose their salvation. That's point one. Point two is that the people in verse 12 are not children of God, they are "children of the kingdom." You say what's the difference? Well, the phrase "children of God" almost always refers to Christians. However, Jesus specifically says, "children of the kingdom," which in this passage refers to the "Jews" – God's chosen people.

Now, during the days of Moses, God made a special promise to the Jews. He promised them that if they would continue to believe (not just believe at some specific point of time in their life, as we do to become a Christian, but continue to believe) that He would one day send them a Messiah. And, if they would continue to obey the laws in the Pentateuch (the first five books of the Bible), they would one day enter into the kingdom of heaven. So, for literally thousands of years, the Jews waited patiently for God to send the Messiah; and now that He was finally here, some of the Jews were rejecting Him.

Therefore, the explanation of Matthew 8:11-12 is that many people, Gentiles from every region of the earth, from every period of time, shall come and sit down with Abraham, Isaac, and Jacob (the Jewish patriarchs) in the kingdom of heaven. But, some of the children of the kingdom, the Jews, shall be cast out of the kingdom of heaven (which was specifically prepared for them) because they rejected their Messiah, who is none other than the Lord Jesus Christ. And they shall be cast into outer darkness, where there shall be weeping and wailing, and gnashing of teeth.

Are you convinced yet? No! Well, let's look at 1 Timothy 4:16. 1 Timothy 4:16 says, "**Take heed unto yourself, and unto the doctrine; continue in them: for in doing this** you shall **both save yourself, and them that hear thee.**" Here we go again. At first glance, it does look like this verse is teaching a Christian can lose their salvation, because Paul is telling Timothy (a minister) **take heed unto yourself** (take care to live a holy life), and, take heed **unto the doctrine** (take care to teach others the truth), for in doing so you shall **both save yourself** and **them that hear thee**.

However, this verse has nothing to do with salvation in the sense of going to heaven to live eternally with God. Would you like to know how I know that? Listen closely to the end of the verse. Paul said, "You shall **both save yourself and them that hear thee.**"

I have two questions for you. First, can a person save himself? I know someone may answer the question by saying "yes." But the answer is "no!" Ephesians 2:8-9 says, "**For by grace ye are saved through faith; and that not of yourselves:** *it is* **the gift of God: not of works, lest anyone should boast.**" God says your salvation is My **gift** to you. And you can't earn a gift! God also says, your salvation is **not of works**. In other words, it's not based on good works such as living a holy life. If you are a Christian, and if you are saved, it is because you were saved by grace through faith. Therefore, no one can save himself.

My second question is this: Can a person save someone else? The obvious answer is no! No one can save another person.

Well, if this is true (and it is), then what in the world did Paul mean when he said, "**Take heed unto yourself, and unto the doctrine; continue in them: for in doing this** you shall **both save yourself, and them that hear thee?**" What did he mean? . . . Well, in order to determine what Paul meant, we must correctly define the key word in the passage, which is "save." The word "save" here means "to deliver from the bondage of sin by God's power through human agency."

What does that mean? That means that God uses people, such as ministers, to warn us and deliver us from the bondage of sin. Thus Paul is telling Timothy, take care to live a holy life, for in doing so you will deliver yourself from the bondage and consequences of sin (e.g., if you don't commit fornication, you will deliver yourself from sexually transmitted diseases). Paul also tells Timothy, take care to teach others the truth, for in doing so you will deliver your congregation from the bondage and consequences of sin, assuming of course they heed your advice (e.g., if you don't commit robbery or theft, you will deliver yourself from the penitentiary). Thus, 1 Timothy 4:16 is dealing with salvation in the sense of deliverance from the bondage of sin in one's life. Not salvation in the sense of being saved from hell through living a holy life.

LET'S EXAMINE A TRULY DIFFICULT PASSAGE

Alright, let's look at one more example. Turn to John 15:6. In this verse Jesus says, **"If a man does not abide in Me, he is cast forth as a branch, and is withered; and men gather them, and cast *them* into the fire, and they are burned."** What did Jesus say? ". . . they are cast into the fire and burned." But I thought you said there's no way we could lose our salvation? I did! Well what does this mean? It means we have to put on our thinking caps. Seriously! This is one of the most difficult passages in all the Bible to interpret.

Now, the first thing we must understand is that in this section of Scripture (John 14:1-16:33) Jesus is talking to the disciples who are living in the Old Testament, but who are also about to enter into the New Testament. The reason why we know this is because Jesus says they will be "in Him," an expression used EXCLUSIVELY to describe Christians (see John 14:20). Therefore, this verse isn't talking about people who "merely profess" to be Christians, as some would teach. This verse is talking about Christians.

Okay, next . . . what is Jesus talking about? Well, in John 15:4-8, Jesus is talking about abiding in Him; which by the way, is the second reason why we know this verse (and this whole section of Scripture) is talking about Christians. I mean think about what Jesus said. If any man, or woman (if any Christian) does not ABIDE in Me, he is "cast forth." Now obviously, this verse can't be talking about a person who has never "received" Jesus Christ as their Lord and Savior, because unbelievers can not abide in Christ!

Now, we just said a moment ago that Jesus is talking about "abiding in Him." This is different than "being in Him." "Being in Christ" has to do with our eternal salvation; "abiding in Christ" has to do with our spiritual nourishment. When a Christian abides in Christ, he receives spiritual nourishment which enables him to bear fruit: the fruit of the Spirit (Galatians 5:22-23), the fruit of righteousness (Hebrews 12:6-11), and the fruit of witnessing (Romans 1:13-15).

Alright, now, how does a Christian abide in Christ? By living his life in obedience to God's Word. Jesus says, "If any man keeps My words (i.e., My commandments), I and My Father will abide with him. I am the vine, the true vine . . . and My Father is the husbandman. You are the branches: he that abides in Me shall bring forth much fruit. But (here it comes), **if a man does not abide in Me, he is cast forth as a branch, and is withered; and men gather them, and cast *them* into the fire, and they are burned** (see John 14:21-23, 15:1-6).

Now, what does this verse mean? Well, it either means a Christian can lose his salvation, or, a Christian can lose his rewards. I have studied this verse many times in my life. And every time I study it I always come back to the same conclusion. . . . This verse is talking about the fact that a Christian can lose his rewards when he gets to heaven. I say this for three reasons.

First, let's remember that the analogy that Christ uses here is dealing with our service for Him. This passage (John 15:1-16) isn't dealing with our salvation, it's dealing with our fruitfulness. Jesus is talking about "abiding in Him." He's talking about bearing "fruit," "more fruit," and "much fruit." Then in verse 16 He says, "You **have not chosen Me, but I have chosen you, and ordained you!**" You see all Christians, not just Ministers, have been ordained by God. All Christians have been anointed by God!

Why? Because God wants all Christians to serve Him in some capacity. God wants all Christians to be involved in ministry. God wants all Christians to bear fruit! Jesus declares, "**I have ordained you** (Christian), that you **should go and bring forth fruit, AND *THAT* YOUR FRUIT SHOULD REMAIN!**" Notice, not your "salvation," your "fruit." You see, some Christian's fruit (i.e., works) will be burned up at the Judgment Seat of Christ. That's why 2 John 1:8 warns us to "**Look to yourselves, that we lose not those things which we have** worked for, **but that we** may **receive a full reward.**"

But wait a minute. What does the last part of the verse mean? ". . . **and men gather them, and cast *them* into the fire, and they are burned.**" That's a good question. And that brings me to my second point. Look at the pronouns in this verse. Verse 6 begins with a singular pronoun: "If A man does not abide;" but it ends with plural pronouns: "and men gather

THEM". . . and "THEY are burned." Why is that? I mean if Jesus was really talking about a Christian going to hell, why didn't He simply say, "if A man does not abide in Me, HE is cast forth as a branch, and men gather HIM, and cast HIM into the fire, and HE is burned?"

Why does Jesus switch to plural pronouns? He didn't do that in Matthew 24:48-51. Nor did He do that in Matthew 25:41-46. (And there are other examples that I could have used.) Now, listen closely. In Matthew 24:48-51 Jesus said, ". . . and **if that evil servant shall say in HIS heart, My lord delays his coming . . . the lord of THAT SERVANT shall come in a day when he is not looking for *him* . . . and shall cut HIM asunder, and appoint *HIM* HIS portion with the hypocrites:** where **there shall be weeping and gnashing of teeth.**" In Matthew 25: 41-46, Jesus warned He will someday say, "**. . . depart from Me, YE cursed . . . for I was hungry, and YE gave Me no meat; I was thirsty, and YE gave Me no drink . . . Then shall THEY answer. . . Lord, when did WE see Thee hungry, or thirsty . . . ? Then He shall answer, Inasmuch as YE did *it* not to one of the least of these, YE did *it* not to Me. And THESE shall go away into everlasting punishment . . .**" Were you listening? In both cases, Jesus either uses all singular pronouns or all plural pronouns. But in John 15:6, Jesus switches from a singular pronoun, to plural pronouns. Why? Why does He say "them". . . and "they?"

Well, I realize this may be difficult for you to understand, but the change in pronouns (from one to many) in this verse demonstrates once again the unmistakable perfection of the words of the Bible. The "them" and the "they" in this verse, represents what a Christian "BEARS" that is "cast forth" and "burned." And what is it that is borne from the life of a Christian who does not abide in Christ? DEAD WORKS (1 Corinthians 3:12 calls this wood, hay, and stubble)! Dead works because they were produced through the energy of the flesh instead of being borne through the power of the Spirit. And what will become of a Christian's "dead works?" 1 Corinthians 3:15 tells us, a Christians "dead works" **shall be burned** (the same Greek word as in John 15:6), and **he shall suffer loss: but he himself shall be saved; yet so as by fire.**"

Lot is a good example of this. When he moved to Sodom he allowed himself to become **conformed to this world** (Romans 12:2). After awhile he began to compromise, and his relationship with the Lord suffered: he no longer stood for holiness, he became a poor father, and he lost his testimony. You see slowly but surely, he became worldly, and he no longer glorified God. Thus, he bore dead works! . . .

Now, when God's judgment rained down upon Sodom, what happened to Lot? Well, all of his works: all the things he lived for, all of his carnal deeds, all of his livestock and all of his material possessions which he had worked for, and, all of his so-called good works which he had done in the flesh . . . all of his unfruitful, dead works – EVERYTHING – was burned up (see 1 Corinthians 3:1-3, Romans 8:6-7, Ephesians 5:11, and Hebrews 9:14). Yet, **he himself** was **saved**.

My third and finally point, which must be understood, is that when John wrote his gospel, he didn't write "**men**" gather them. If you were to look at the Greek text you'd discover he actually wrote "**they**" gather them. To see the significance of this we must turn to Matthew 13:41-42. It reads, "**The Son of Man shall send forth His angels and they shall gather out of His kingdom all things that offend, and them which do iniquity: and shall cast them into a furnace of fire: there shall be wailing and gnashing of teeth.**"

Now, this is important. Please note that the angels cast TWO THINGS into the fire: "**all things that offend**" (i.e., a Christian's dead works) and "**them which do iniquity**" (i.e., unsaved sinners). Therefore, the correct interpretation of John 15:6 is that a Christians "dead works" will be burned up at the Judgment Seat of Christ (Romans 14:10 and 1 Corinthians 3:10-15). Needless to say, unsaved sinners will be cast into the lake of fire at the Great White Throne Judgment (Revelation 20:11-15).

Therefore, what we have here in verse 6 is a truly sobering admonition that we should heed. Listen, either you and I will choose to abide in Christ and, as a result of our abiding, we will bear much fruit, or, we will choose not to abide in Christ; to do our own thing, go our own way. But if we choose not to abide in Christ, there is the very real possibility that we will one day stand before the Lord Jesus Christ and watch all of our so-called good works go up in smoke.

Dear Christian friend, is that what you really want? To do your own thing, and not allow God to use you to witness, and teach, and minister to others! Do you really want to wake up someday in the future, only to realize that you've wasted your whole life! And then, to top everything off, come before the Lord Jesus (whom you say that you love) and try to explain to Him why you didn't abide in Him. Why you didn't live your life for Him. My friend, wouldn't you rather abide in Christ? Wouldn't you like to hear Jesus say, "Well done, thou good and faithful servant? . . . Oh I know sometimes it won't be easy! But wouldn't you rather abide in Christ and bring forth fruit, more fruit, and much fruit! Wouldn't you rather live your life knowing, for all eternity, that your life mattered! That you made a difference because you abided in Christ! And as a result, people's lives were changed! Isn't THAT what you really want? Then I encourage you, in fact I challenge you, to abide in Christ.

The Issue of
Eternal Security
(Part Two)

CHAPTER THREE

Last week we began studying the very controversial issue of "eternal security." Eternal security is one of the many doctrines of the Christian faith. Briefly stated this doctrine teaches that once a person truly receives Jesus Christ as their personal Lord and Savior, they can never be lost.

Now, if you will remember, in the introduction last week I asked two critical questions which must be pondered if one is going to seriously study this issue. The first question was this. Does God provide salvation, or does man do something to obtain salvation? I mean in the final analysis, does God save us, or do we contribute something to our own salvation? The second question was this. Are the saved promised eternal life, or a chance to receive eternal life? In other words, does God give the Christian eternal life, with no strings attached? Or does God give eternal life, stipulating that we have to live right to keep it? These are very, very important questions we need to ponder, and I invite you to do that as we conclude this lesson today.

So far, we've spent the majority, of our time looking at those verses which people commonly use to try to teach that a Christian can lose his salvation. I want to pick up right there, right where we left off last week, and I want us to look at a few more of these passages before we turn our attention to the Scriptures which prove – beyond a shadow of a doubt – that when a "Christian" dies, they will spend eternity with God in heaven.

MORE CONTROVERSIAL PASSAGES

Please turn to the Gospel of Matthew. In verses 31 and 32 of chapter 12, Jesus says, "**Wherefore I say unto you, All manner of sin and blasphemy shall be forgiven unto men: but the blasphemy** *against* **the** *Holy* **Spirit shall not be forgiven unto men. And whosoever speaks a word against the Son of Man, it shall be forgiven him: but whosoever speaks against the Holy Spirit, it shall not be forgiven him, neither in this world, neither in the** *world* **to come."**

This passage deals with what is commonly called "the unpardonable sin." If a person commits the unpardonable sin Jesus says he will die and go to hell. Because of this, many people teach that if a Christian commits the unpardonable sin he will lose his salvation.

Question, what is "the unpardonable sin?" Many people think it is when a person commits suicide, because they say if a person commits suicide he can't ask God for forgiveness. Others believe it is speaking against the Holy Spirit: that is, saying something derogatory about the Holy Spirit, or mocking

Him, or cursing Him. Many ministers teach that it is when a person lives their whole life refusing to accept Christ as their personal Savior. While this is an unpardonable sin, it is not "the" unpardonable sin spoken of in this passage. In my earlier days I used to believe and actually taught this view.

Now while all of these interpretations have been used to explain this passage throughout the years, none of them are correct. So the question remains, "What is the unpardonable sin?" "What is blasphemy against the Holy Spirit?" Well, it is saying (and believing) that the miracles Jesus Christ did through the power of the Holy Spirit, while He was here on earth, were actually done through the power of Satan (please read Matthew 12:15-37 and Mark 3:13-30). Now, since this is the true interpretation of the passage, no one can commit this sin today, because Jesus is no longer physically here on earth.

You see, in order for a person to commit the unpardonable sin, blasphemy against the Holy Spirit, they would have had to: 1) been alive when Jesus Christ was physically here on earth; 2) known the Old Testament Messianic Scriptures like Isaiah 61:1-2; 3) seen Jesus perform the miracles He did; and 4) told Jesus He has an unclean spirit (read John 8:12-59). This is exactly what many of the Jewish religious leaders did. They "knew" the Scriptures. They "saw" Jesus cure every sickness, cast out every kind of demon, and heal every kind of physical deformity. And yet, in spite of all the evidence, they said, "Jesus has an unclean spirit!" They claimed that the Lord Jesus Christ was performing miracles through the power, or agency of Satan, rather than the Holy Spirit. Can you imagine seeing Jesus feeding the 5,000, giving sight to the blind, healing the lame, raising the dead, and casting out demons? Can you imagine seeing Jesus performing the miracles the Scriptures prophesied the Messiah would do and then saying to Jesus, "You have an unclean spirit, you are demon possessed, you are performing these miracles through the power of Satan!" Can you picture that? That's what many of the Jewish religious leaders did, and because of that, when they died they went to hell.

Now obviously, since Jesus is no longer physically here, since Jesus has ascended into heaven, no one can commit this sin today.

Let's move on to the next passage. Turn to Philippians 2:12. Paul says, "**Wherefore, my beloved, as ye have always obeyed, not as in my presence only, but now much more in my absence, work out your own salvation with fear and trembling.**" Alright, here's another verse people use to say, "See here, you have to work for your salvation. Or, even if we are saved by grace, we have to work to keep it." But again, this verse doesn't teach that. Did you read the verse? Paul didn't say work "for" your salvation. Nor did he say work "in order that you might keep" your own salvation. Paul said work "out" your salvation. What does he mean? What is the correct interpretation of this verse? . . . Well, Paul is saying, because you are already saved, and because you have the power of the Spirit of God at work within you – now, outwardly, demonstrate that you are saved by your conduct.

Now of course, nobody can work their salvation out unless God has already worked it in. Right? Therefore, Paul's point here is simply this. Work out your salvation: demonstrate to this **crooked and perverse nation** that you are sons (and daughters) of the living God – holy and blameless! Don't murmur and dispute among yourselves. Be united! And live holy lives! **Shine as lights in the world!** And don't do it in your own strength, nor in the energy of the flesh. Do it through the power of the Holy Spirit which is at work within you (see Philippians 2:13-15).

One more thing. Paul said do this, **with fear and trembling**. What does Paul mean? Why should we **work out** our salvation **with fear and trembling**? Because your life is the only Bible that some people will ever read. . . . People are looking at you. Unbelievers are watching YOU! They are checking you out to see if you are walking the walk. Anybody can talk the talk. People are looking at you! And based on how you live, they are deciding whether or not God is real! Because (they think) if God is real you're not going to cuss people out. You're not going to commit adultery, or fornication. You're not going to gossip, or look at pornography, or get drunk, or lie, or cheat on your income tax form. They think you should live differently! Why? Because you're a Christian! And if we don't live differently than non-believers, why should they become a Christian. After all, we're all nothing but a bunch of hypocrites! Right? And if that's what Christianity really is, I don't need that, and I don't need God! Because God isn't real! Because if God was real, you wouldn't be living like that!

You see, we need to "**work out**" our salvation "**with fear and trembling**," because people are watching us. Whether we realize it or not, we are affecting peoples lives. And unfortunately, some people are going to choose whether or not to receive Jesus Christ as their Savior based on how we live.

Let me remind you of something I said last week. You must get this issue of eternal security settled in your life, because it is the starting point of true spiritual maturity! This is the starting point of true Christian service! You cannot grow into full and complete maturity, as a Christian, until you settle this issue in your life. In fact, until this issue is settled your spiritual growth will be stunted. Your spiritual growth will be impeded, both intellectually and emotionally, causing you to grow abnormally: causing you to serve God out of fear instead of love.

My point is obvious. Satan has convinced some Christians into believing that they might actually be cast into hell. And therefore, they serve God out of fear: they are trying to live right because they fear God will cast them into hell. . . . They're fearing the wrong thing! Paul said, **"work out"** your salvation **"with fear and trembling,"** because you are God's witnesses. You are God's ambassadors. And ultimately, some people are going to choose whether or not to receive Christ based on how we live.

Do you see also how their whole motivation for serving God is wrong? If I don't serve God and keep His commandments, He will cast me into hell. That's not the reason why we should serve God. Again, we should serve God and keep His commandments because if we don't we might cause some unbeliever to be cast into hell. Because they may look at how we live our life and go one of two ways. As I said earlier, based on how we live they may come to the conclusion that Christianity is a sham, and choose not to receive Christ. Or, they may think, "I live better than he does. I live better than she does. If they're going to heaven, then I know I'm going to heaven!" Not realizing, of course, that the only reason WHY we're going to heaven is because all our sins have been forgiven: because we've received the Lord Jesus Christ by faith.

Still with me? Well look at Galatians 5:19-21. Paul says, **"Now the works of the flesh are manifest, which are *these*; adultery, fornication, uncleanness, lasciviousness, idolatry, witchcraft, hatred, variance, emulations, wrath, strife, seditions, heresies, envyings, murders, drunkenness, revellings, and such like: of the which I tell you beforehand, as I have also told *you* in time past, that they which do such things shall not inherit the kingdom of God."**

Okay, I have to admit, at first glance it does look like this passage is teaching a Christian can lose their salvation. Because verse 21 says if you do these, or similar sins, you **shall not inherit the kingdom of God**. I must also admit that this passage is the one that used to scare me to death!

When you come to a passage like this you really must pray and ask God to give you wisdom to be able to interpret it correctly. But after you pray, what do you do? I mean where do you start? Well, a good place to start would be to define the "key" word or words in the passage. What is the key word in this passage? That little word "do." What does "do" mean? The word "do" comes from the Greek word "prassontes," and it means "to practice." Now that, THAT, is a very important tidbit of information – because you see, a Christian can and does commit sin. Sometimes, a Christian even commits the sins listed in this passage. And if he or she does, they can always be confessed and forgiven. Praise God (see 1 John 1:9)! But a Christian can not practice sin. "Practice" refers to doing something over and over again; to do continually and repeatedly; to do as a normal, customary, manner of conduct. Now obviously, if a Christian is in a bad marriage they may yield to temptation and commit adultery. But, a Christian cannot "practice," that is commit adultery over and over and over and over and over again as a NORMAL way of life. . . .

Which brings me to the really hard part of discussing the issue of sin in the life of a believer. I pray that this doesn't confuse you, and I also pray that God will give you insight into what I'm saying, so that you will know I'm speaking the truth.

The first thing we must understand, is that "there is a distinction" between those who "practice sin" and those who "sin habitually?" Now, I know that this will seem a bit confusing at first. But a distinction must be made. For I do realize that there are some Christians who are caught in habitual sin. They are caught in habitual sin, because they do not know how to appropriate the power of the Holy Spirit, or resist temptation. Now, when I say "habitual" I mean sinful behavior that, through the process of time, has become nearly or completely involuntary (see the apostle Paul's description of this in Romans 7:14-24). I hope and pray that you can truly grasp this distinction, because this is definitely a little different than freely choosing to practice sin.

For those who may be caught in this situation take heart. There are several good Christian books that deal with "How to Be Filled with the Spirit," "How to Walk in the Spirit," "How to Put On (and wear) the Whole Armor of God," "How to Resist Temptation," and "How to Fight Temptation," which you can buy in many Christian Bookstores. I have also written booklets on these subjects. If you wish, you may write and request them.

I should also point out that some Christians, who are carnal, simply choose to live in sin. Now, I know that many will disagree with me at this point, because a lot of people don't believe a Christian can live in sin. But based on the interpretation of Hebrews 6:4-6 (which we discussed in the last chapter), it is possible for a Christian to live in sin. This brings up the obvious question, "What's the difference between a non-Christian who practices sin, and a Christian who lives in sin?" Well, the difference is it's NORMAL for an unbeliever to practice sin. It's not normal for a Christian to live in sin. That's why, generally speaking, the non-Christian (i.e., the Natural Man) is less miserable than the Carnal Christian: it's because the Carnal Christian doesn't experience joy (see 1 Corinthians 2:14-3:3 and Psalm 51:12).

There is also one more difference which I should touch on. In the New Testament Church Age (which we're now living in) God reproves unbelievers (John 16:7-11), but He rebukes Christians (Hebrews 12:5-11). You say, "What's the difference?" Well, when God reproves an unbeliever He usually scolds or corrects them gently, with kindly intent. He lovingly convicts them, because He is not willing that any should perish. His desire is that all would come to repentance (see 2 Peter 3:9). On the other hand, when a Christian chooses to live in sin, the Lord rebukes them. He lovingly, but sharply, reprimands them and severely disciplines them, because they should know better! Instead of living in sin, they should be abiding in Christ! Why? Well, let me break it down for you. If a Christian obeys God, serves God, worships God, and glorifies God, GOD WILL BLESS THEM: both in this life, and, in the life to come (see Matthew 6:33 and Mark 10:28-30). But, as we shall see later, if a Christian chooses to live in sin, they will pay dearly . . . they will, pay, dearly!

All right, let's turn to Matthew one more time. Matthew 24:13 says, **"But he that shall endure unto the end, the same shall be saved."** Here again, this is another one of those verses that people have misinterpreted down through the centuries. They say if a Christian doesn't hold out till the end, or remain faithful to Christ till the end of his life, he won't be saved.

However, if you read the entire chapter you'll see that Jesus isn't talking about Christians here. He's talking about people who will be living on the earth during the Tribulation Period, which is after (not before) the Rapture of the Church. The reason why I say the Rapture will take place before the tribulation is because 1 Thessalonians 1:9-10 says ". . . **ye turned to God from idols to serve the living and true God; and to wait for His Son from heaven, whom He raised from the dead,** *even* **Jesus, which delivered us from the wrath to come.**" Notice, the verse is in the past tense. Jesus has already **delivered us from the wrath to come.**

What's going to happen when the Tribulation Period comes? God is going to pour out His wrath upon the world! Revelation 15:1-16:21 says the world (i.e., Jews, Gentiles, the unsaved, and, tribulation believers) will experience the wrath of God. But 1 Thessalonians 1:9-10 says, "WE" (Christians) have been delivered **from the wrath to come**: this would indicate that the rapture will take place before the Tribulation Period begins.

Thus, 1 Thessalonians 5:9 says, "**For God has not appointed us to wrath . . .**" You see, God's divine wrath against "us" (because of our sins) has already been taken away, because Jesus Christ took our place on the cross and paid (past tense) the penalty for all our sins. Therefore, "WE" (Christians), will not experience **the wrath to come**.

Now, when the Rapture takes place, all Christians will leave the earth, and go to be with the Lord in heaven (see 1 Thessalonians 4:13-17). When this occurs, the only people who will be left on earth will be the unbelieving Jews and unbelieving Gentiles. After this the Tribulation Period will begin. And during this time, God will pour out His wrath upon the world. Now, during this time many people will turn to Jesus and receive Him as their Savior/Messiah. But because there will be no assurance of eternal life during the Tribulation Period these "tribulation believers" will have to endure many tests, and trials, and temptations in order to be saved.

You must realize we live in a unique age, in a unique dispensation. Today people are saved by grace, through faith. But when the Rapture takes place, it will mark the end of the Church Age. When the "Church Age" ends, the "age of grace" will end. Now that doesn't mean tribulation believers won't be saved by grace. They will be. But, it means they wont be saved by grace, through faith, ALONE! Tribulation believers (i.e., people who receive Jesus Christ during the tribulation) will be saved by grace, through faith, plus works. They will have to perform good works until the Second Coming of Christ in order to REMAIN SAVED: good works such as not taking the mark of the beast, helping the Jews escape the antichrist, dying for Christ without renouncing Him, etc.

SOME GUIDELINES TO FOLLOW

Obviously, there are many other verses that people use to try to prove that a Christian can lose his salvation, but these are some of the more common ones. Now, rather than take up more time explaining more verses, let me just give you some guidelines on how to study the Bible, so that when you come across verses such as these you'll be able to interpret them correctly.

- First pray. Ask God to explain to you what the passage or verse means.

- Second, study the surrounding context of the passage.

- Third, determine who the verses are written to (e.g., Jews, Gentiles, the unsaved, Old Testament believers, Christians, or tribulation believers).

- Fourth, find out what time period (or dispensation) is being discussed (e.g., Old Testament, New Testament, Church Age, Tribulation Period, or the Millennial Kingdom).

- Fifth, study the words of the passage or verse very carefully. I would even suggest using Hebrew and Greek Dictionaries, Webster's Collegiate Dictionary, and Strong's Exhaustive Concordance to find out the meaning of "key" words and phrases.

• Sixth, in some cases you may need to seek understanding from other sources, such as reliable in-depth Bible commentaries, or qualified teachers of the Bible whom you trust.

• Seventh, if you still don't understand the meaning of the verse after you've studied it, wait patiently for the Holy Spirit to reveal it to you. Once I had to wait six months for God to show me the explanation of a verse. Honestly, I just couldn't figure it out. Then one day, out of the blue, God just opened up my understanding.

VERSES THAT PROVE WE'RE SECURE

So far, we have looked at some of the verses which people use to try to prove that a Christian can lose their eternal life. Now, let's turn our attention to those verses which prove beyond any shadow of a doubt that a Christian is eternally secure.

First, turn to John 6:37. Jesus says, **"All that the Father gives Me shall come to Me; and him that comes to Me I will in no wise cast out."** What did Jesus say? "I will in no wise cast out." What? "I will in no wise cast out!" Now honestly, if there was the slightest possibility that we could lose our salvation don't you think Jesus would have said, "him that comes to Me I will in no wise cast out, UNLESS he commits murder, or idolatry, or rape, or some other horrible sin." But notice, no stipulations. Notice too that this verse is talking about "Christians" who live in "this age," because technically speaking, except for the disciples, the Father didn't give anyone to Jesus until after He died on the cross. You see, it was there

68

that He paid the price, and bought us with His life (1 Peter 1:18-19 and 1 Corinthians 6:19-20; see also Mark 9:30-41 and John 17:5-12). All the disciples (except for Judas) represent "the Church," even though the Church Age doesn't begin until Acts 2. Remember, the word "Church" means "called out ones." The disciples were "called out" in Mark 3:13-19.

All right, the next passage I want you to look at is Ephesians 1:13. The apostle Paul says, we "**were sealed with that holy Spirit of promise.**" When a person receives Christ they are sealed with the Holy Spirit. This brings to mind a great analogy. Imagine for a moment that you have just written a very important letter. What would you normally do with that letter? Well, you would place it in an envelope, securely seal it up, address it, put a stamp on it, and then – you would mail it.

Well, in the same way, when a person receives Jesus Christ they become God's letter (i.e., God's epistle) (see 2 Corinthians 3:1-3). Then they are placed inside Jesus, who is the envelope (John 14:20), and sealed with the Holy Spirit. For how long? **Unto the day of redemption** (see Ephesians 4:30). Now, if the envelope is securely sealed, there is no way it will flop open, and thus allow the letter to fall out. Right? Well notice, the Holy Spirit is the glue which seals the envelope. You can't get a more sure seal than that, can you? . . . Therefore, a Christian cannot fall out of Christ. He might "fall away" from Christ, in the sense of Hebrews 6:4-6 which we saw earlier, but he can never "fall out" of Christ.

Now, when an envelope is sealed no one can legally open it until it reaches its destination. Nor can the letter, of its own free will or power, break the seal and get out of the envelope. Isn't that true? Well then tell me, is there anyone, any being in all the universe, that has the legal authority or power to open up the envelope (which is Christ) and take you out before it reaches heaven? NO! . . . Well, can a Christian of his own free will or power break the seal and get out? Of course not. Then how can you lose your salvation? You see, you can't. To finish the analogy, you have already been addressed (see Revelation 3:12 and 1 John 5:4-5), and the postage has already been paid (see Acts 20:28 and Colossians 1:13-14); you're just waiting now for the "mailman" to come (see 1 Corinthians 1:7 and 1 Thessalonians 4:13-17).

Okay, turn back to the Gospel of John. In John 10:28-29 Jesus said, "**I give unto them eternal life; and they shall never perish, neither shall anyone pluck them out of My hand. My Father, which gave *them* to Me, is greater than all; and no one is able to pluck *them* out of My Father's hand.**"

Once again, the first thing you notice about this passage is what it doesn't say. There are no conditions, no terms. Jesus doesn't say, "I will give them eternal life if they continue to obey the Ten Commandments." Jesus doesn't say, "if they continually perform good works they shall never perish." Jesus simply says, "I give them eternal life". . . no strings attached.

Jesus goes on to say, no one can pluck them out of My hand, or My Father's hand. The Christian is secure in God's hand: Satan and all his demons put together do not have the power to pry God's fingers apart to snatch you out; and you, dear Christian, do not have the strength to wriggle your way out of God's hand. And, just so there would be no doubt whatsoever, Jesus said I will never cast you out (see John 6:37-40). Now if that doesn't assure you that you will spend eternity with God in heaven, nothing will.

WHAT ABOUT LOOSE LIVING

If I wanted, I could share with you many other verses which prove we are secure. But, it is my hope that you realize now you can never be lost if you are a Christian. This logically leads us to my next point, which I should at least touch on before I conclude. And that is the issue of loose living.

The reason why a lot of people don't discuss eternal security is because they know some Christians will begin to think, "Hey, since I'm a Christian and can never lose my salvation, that means I can sin as much as I want. And do anything I want to do." WRONG! If any of you are beginning to think like that I have a word of warning for you. . . . Don't try it, you won't like it! You won't get away with it!!! . . . If you get involved in willful sin, if you deliberately disobey God, you will pay dearly. For while it is true that you will not lose your salvation, you may lose everything else.

You see, when a Christian sins, he grieves and quenches the Holy Spirit (Ephesians 4:30 and 1 Thessalonians 5:19). In other words, he saddens the Holy Spirit and stifles Him. Now when this happens, when a Christian sins, he looses fellowship with God (1 John 1:6-7). Do you know what happens when you loose fellowship with God? God stops blessing you (Psalm 84:11), and God stops answering your prayers (Psalm 66:18).

Now, if a Christian doesn't confess his sin and ask for forgiveness at this point, but continues to disobey God, the next thing he will lose is his joy (Psalm 51:12). God will take away the joy of his salvation and he will become miserable. Thus, instead of experiencing the joy of the Lord, he will experience depression, anxiety, worry, sorrow, and fear. . . .

Now, if he doesn't confess his sin and ask for forgiveness at this point, but defiantly continues to disobey, God has three final options. God can either put him on the shelf, which means he will lose his testimony and, as a result, be mocked by unbelievers, as well as become a stumbling block to potential converts (see Matthew 5:13-16, Philippians 2:14-15, and 1 Corinthians 5:1-13); or, God can make him weak and sickly; or, God can kill him, which means he will lose his life (see 1 Corinthians 11:23-32, 1 John 5:14-16, and Acts 5:1-11).

THE EXAMPLE OF THE CORINTHIANS

1 Corinthians 11:23-32 is a sobering example of this. Do you remember what happened in Corinth? When the Christians came to celebrate the Lord's Supper, they brought food to have a feast: to share a meal (i.e., to spend time in fellowship with one another) before communion took place. Of course, in the church of Corinth there were rich and poor: there were those who could bring plenty; there were those who could bring very little; and there were even slaves who could bring nothing. Thus, for the poor and slaves, this might have been the only truly decent meal they would have been able to have until the next time they celebrated the Lord's Supper.

However, sin crept in and things went horribly wrong at these feasts. For whatever reason, these Christians stopped sharing their food. The rich would literally eat their food and gorge themselves, while the poor and slaves ate next to nothing. Can you imagine that? One person is sitting in the room with barely a crust of bread. And sitting right next to him is a person who is eating sumptuously, who won't share his food. And when you think about the fact that these were Christians! . . . I mean this was an incredibly carnal and sad picture. And to make things worse, some of the folks were getting drunk!

Well the result, was that this feast, which was supposed to demonstrate the fact that "in Christ" differences (such as class, and nationality, and race, and gender) were now eliminated, only succeeded in exacerbating them. This feast, which was supposed to foster unity, only succeeded in creating more disunity. I mean the Lord's Supper was suppose to bring Christians into closer fellowship with one another, as they remembered Jesus' sacrifice for them and looked forward to His return. But how can you have true fellowship with one another when some are starving, some are satiated, and some are drunk?

So Paul said that because they were shaming those who had very little; thus in effect, despising the church of God: that many of them (not just some, but many of them) were weak, and sickly, and, many of them had fallen asleep. And when the Bible uses the word "sleep" like that, it's not talking about gettin' some z's. It means some of them had died. You see, when the word "sleep" is used in that way, it is a euphemism for death. Thus, what he was saying to the Corinthians was that God had brought judgment upon them: and because of that, many of them were weak, many of them were sickly, and many of them had died.

Here's the reality. Because of their stinginess and carnality, many of them died. But I want you to notice something. God didn't say, "I sent some of them to hell." In other words, they didn't lose their salvation. When God redeems us by the blood of Christ, He doesn't then somehow make us unborn spiritually because we sin. But, we can come under the judgment of God for our carnality, for our disobedience.

Listen, if you willfully, continuously, unrepentantly, rebel against God – even though you have been saved – you will fall under the judgment of God just as the Corinthians did. They fell under God's judgment because of their sin, even though they were saved. They never lost their salvation, but they never reached spiritual maturity because they chose to live in sin . . . because they chose to walk in the flesh. And because of that they never experienced what Jesus calls the abundant life, even though they had been redeemed from sin's slavery, and redeemed from sin's penalty. You see 1 Corinthians 11:23-32, 1 John 5:14-16, and Acts 5:1-11 are a warning against choosing to go into rebellion and disobedience.

You see, when you choose to live in rebellion against God, again, and again, and again, and again, you come to that place where you harden your heart. And at that point, God either puts you on the shelf, or He allows you to become weak and sickly, or, He kills you. When you repeatedly resist the Holy Spirit, and repeatedly choose not to repent of your sin, there comes a point when God says, "Okay, I'm going to leave you in your sin, or, I'm going to bring you home, even though I wanted you to live on the earth for many more years." And at that moment you seal your fate, not eternally, but temporally.

I hope and pray that you truly grasp this. Because these Scriptures are examples meant to warn us. What does the Scriptures say? God doesn't change (see James 1:17): He's the same yesterday, today, and forever. If this happened to those first century Christians, it can happen to us today.

IF YOU SEE YOUR BROTHER SIN

Now, I know this can be difficult for some of you to stomach: because some of you have family members who once professed to be Christians. But boy, they're not living like it today. And you say to yourself, what can I do? Pray for them. And lovingly talk to them: plead with them to repent, because

74

nobody knows when God's going to say, "Okay, you've reached the point of no return.

1 John 5:16 says, "**If any man see his brother sin a sin** . . . Now again, what's the context? He calls him a "brother." In other words, this isn't a lost person that's sinning. It's a Christian. So, if any man see his brother (a Christian) **sin a sin *which is* not unto death, he shall ask** . . . Ask what? Ask for God to bring him to his senses. Who knows, maybe God will deliver him from his willful disobedience, and from his carnality. After all, God is patient, and long suffering. But look at what the rest of the verse says, "**. . . there is a sin unto** (i.e., that leads to) **death**."

Now, you and I don't know when that is. We don't know when someone is going to reach that point of no return. Therefore, we should keep right on praying for them because only God knows. The point is, if a redeemed person lives continually, and perpetually, in rebellion against God – unrepentant! – they are now taking their life into their own hands. And what that means is, when a redeemed person willfully continues in sin, the judgment of God will come . . . not might, WILL come! Now listen, they're not in danger of losing their salvation – spiritually; but they are in danger of losing their life – physically.

Now (listen carefully) there are some people who don't live like Christians, even though they say they're Christians. And the reason why they don't live like Christians, even though they say they're Christians, is because they're not Christians. Many famous Christian evangelicals have estimated that as many as 60% of church members in America are not truly born again. . . . They profess Christ, but they do not truly possess Christ. They've been baptized, but they've never been born again. They've never become that "new creature" that 2

Corinthians 5:17 talks about. They've never, by faith, received Jesus Christ as their personal Lord and Savior.

You know, sometimes we wonder. "You know so and so, man he came down front, he prayed the prayer, and it looked like he got saved. He made a profession of faith, he got baptized; and you know, for a couple of years we'd see him in church. But man, it looks like he's gone back to his old life. I wonder if he truly got saved?" Well, the reality is, we don't know. Maybe he didn't! . . . Maybe he didn't genuinely believe. Maybe he didn't pray in faith. Or, maybe he was just faking it, with some ulterior motive in mind (e.g., like trying to date a Christian girl he was attracted to).

On the other hand, based on what we're learning, maybe he really did get saved. And now, as a redeemed person he's living in rebellion, living in sin.

We just don't know.

I mean, the only two people that know (that truly know) if a person got saved or not, is that person . . . and God.

But if he is saved and if he is living in rebellion, pray for him, talk to him, and warn him. Because God knows whether he's saved or not. And if he is saved, God is lovingly rebuking him, and chastening him, and scourging him (see Hebrews 12:5-11). God is trying to bring him to his senses through the power of the Holy Spirit that lives within him.

Therefore, if you've been born again, if you're saved, if you've asked the Lord Jesus Christ to come into your heart and life by faith, you're not going to be unborn as a child of God. Why? Because all your sins have been forgiven, because God can't lie, because you've been placed into the body of Christ, and, because you've been adopted into the family of God. But listen very carefully: while you cannot lose your salvation, if you sin willfully and unrepentantly, you are in danger of losing everything else.

Now, you may think I'm trying to scare you, and you may think God doesn't do that anymore. But I do know the true story of a guy whom God took away from here prematurely, because he continued to live in sin.

But that's not the end of it. Oh no! You see after you die, you will then lose most if not all the rewards you could have had, because you chose to continue in sin! And I don't even have time to deal with that consequence! . . . I'm serious! There are very real earthly and eternal consequences when a Christian chooses to rebel against God (see 2 Corinthians 5:9-11 and 1 Corinthians 3:9-15). Can you imagine, living for all eternity; rejoicing on the one hand because you're saved; but on the other hand, regretting the fact that you lost most of your rewards because you disobeyed God?

Now, with all that to look forward to, tell me, do you REALLY want to continue in sin? Do you really want to rebel? I didn't think so. Therefore, when you realize you've committed a sin repent. Don't rebel. Simply repent. Ask God to forgive you. . . . Don't harden your heart against God. Humble yourself before the Lord, and ask Him for forgiveness. Do not use your freedom, your liberty, as an opportunity to sin. Not even occasionally. But through love, serve the Lord and one another (see Romans 6:1-23 and Galatians 5:13-14).

YOU CAN BE SURE

In conclusion then, let me leave you with the passage I began with. The passage my friend shared with me.

> "If we receive the witness of men, the witness of God is greater: for this is the witness of God which He has testified of His Son. He that believes on the Son of God has the witness in himself: he that does not believe God has made Him a liar; because he has not believed the record that God gave of His Son. And this is the record, that God has given to us eternal life, and this life is in His Son. He that has the Son has life; *and* he that does not have the Son of God does not have life. These things I have written unto you that believe on the name of the Son of God; in order that you may know that you have eternal life . . ." (see 1 John 5:9-13)

The apostle John says, "If we receive the witness of men, the witness of God is greater . . ." Do people receive the witness of men? Of course they do. We all do! For example, I'm sure that most of us here have taken a wrong turn someplace and gotten lost before, right? Well, what did you do? You asked a stranger for directions. And what did you do after you received those directions? You followed them to the letter. Even though you didn't know him, you did exactly what he said. You followed his directions and reached your destination. Most of us have, at some time, asked a doctor or friend which medicine they thought would be better to take. What did you do? You listened to their advice, and you went out and bought that particular brand and used it. A few of us have even been summoned to jury duty. What did you do? You paid attention to the testimony of total strangers, you determined whether the defendant was innocent or guilty, and then you rendered a verdict.

Now, in all these cases what were you doing? You were receiving the witness of men! Well, look at what John says. . . . **"If we receive the witness of men, the witness of God is greater."** Why? Because God can't lie! Therefore, we should receive the witness of God. If a person doesn't receive the witness of God he is calling God a liar, because he does not believe the record (or testimony) that God gives concerning His Son Jesus Christ. Well, what has God testified concerning His Son? **This is the record** (in other words, for the record) **God has given to us,** "Christians," **eternal life, and this life is in His Son.**

Now don't rush ahead to the next verse. Think about that for a minute. God gives a person eternal life the very moment he or she receives Christ. Therefore, **"he that has the Son has life; *and* he that does not have the Son of God does not have life."** Did you know that?

Over the years I have asked countless people if they were sure they would spend eternity in heaven. I remember once, I was witnessing to this guy and I asked him that question. His response was classic. He answered, "I don't know, but I sure am working on it." Working on it? You can't work on it! Notice, one last time, John makes no mention of keeping the Ten Commandments, performing good works, living right, or being baptized. You either have received the Son, and by virtue of that fact, you have eternal life; or you haven't received the Son and you don't have eternal life. It's just that simple. Finally, John says, **"These things I have written unto you that believe on the name of the Son of God; in order that** you **may know"** – not hope, or wonder about, or fret over – I have written, **"that** you **may KNOW that** you **have eternal life . . ."**

79

My dear friend, if you have received Christ, if you have asked Jesus Christ by faith to forgive your sins, come into your life, and be your personal Lord and Savior, you can be absolutely sure that you have eternal life. You can be absolutely, positively, 100% sure . . . sure beyond any shadow of a doubt that when you die, you will be ushered into the presence of Jesus to spend all of eternity with Him.

Can We
Be Sure We're
Going to Heaven?

CHAPTER FOUR

Before we begin, I want you to know that we are really going to get deep into the Word of God in this chapter. What I'm going to share with you is going to sound a little strange, a little weird. And I dare venture to say, that some of the things I'm going to share with you, you've probably never ever heard before.

The things I'm going to be sharing with you today are things I learned back when I attended a Bible Institute and Bible College. And of course, some of these things I've learned from pastors. I want you to know, it's taken me a considerable amount of time to actually study these things, and come to the conclusions I've reached. But let me assure you that what I am about to share with you, is common knowledge among many pastors. And I would say, is absolutely true!

So, are you ready to jump into the deep end of Scripture?

Okay, here we go. . . .

One of the most difficult things for us to do is picture ourselves dead, lying in a casket, about to be placed six feet under the earth. The reason why, is because we're all, to some degree, afraid of death. So do you know what we do? We simply choose not to think about it. I mean death can be scary to think about, because in the last few moments of our life, we all have to deal with the inevitable question. Will the Lord allow me, to enter through those pearly gates, into the heavenly city? Or, will He cast me into hell, into unquenchable fire?

WE NEED NOT FEAR

But do you know what the Scriptures say? **For God has not given us the spirit of fear; but of power, and of love, and of a sound mind** (2 Timothy 1:7). Who wrote those words? The apostle Paul. But did he understand what he was saying? Did he REALLY know what he was talking about? YES, he did! . . . And if Paul were here today, I'm sure he'd tell you that before he received Jesus Christ as his Lord and Savior, there was some part of him that was afraid of death. But after he became a Christian do you know what happened to him? In the year 44 or 45 A.D., while he was ministering in Lystra, he was stoned to death! At least the people who cast stones at him thought that they had killed him. They were so sure that he was dead that they dragged his body out of the city (see Acts 14:1-20).

Now, I don't know if the apostle Paul was killed and resurrected, or if he was just given a very bad concussion. But it would seem to me that if the people dragged him out of the city, they would have noticed if he was still breathing or not. Because of this, I personally lean towards the belief that Paul was killed, and then resurrected. But there's no way of knowing for sure. . . . What we do know for sure, is that while Paul was dead (or unconscious), he was transported up into the third heaven (i.e., the abode of God).[1]

Paul describes this experience in 2 Corinthians 12:1-7. (At first glance it appears that Paul is talking about someone else, because he writes in the third person. But he is just being modest, for when you get down to verse 7, it becomes clear that he's speaking about himself.) He says in verses 3 and 4 that when this happened he couldn't tell if he was in his body or out of his body. All he knew was that he found himself in paradise. Paul was literally caught up into heaven.

Now, since Paul's physical body was laying on the ground in Lystra, we must conclude that Paul was in some sort of spiritual body in heaven. (Notice, I didn't say he was in his glorified body. No Christian will receive their glorified body until the rapture takes place, which is described in 1 Thessalonians 4:13-18.) In other words, Paul's body was on earth, but his soul and spirit were in heaven. It is also important to realize that even though Paul was in some sort of spiritual body, he could see, and hear, and speak, and feel, and smell, and think!

Paul said in verse 4, "I **heard unspeakable words, which it is not lawful for a man to utter.**" Wow! Can you imagine what he heard? Can you imagine what he saw? But the Lord

---

[1] Biblically speaking, the first heaven consists of the clouds and our atmosphere. The second heaven is what we would call the universe consisting of the sun, moon, stars, and planets in our solar system, as well as all the other galaxies in outer space. The third heaven is where the Father lives; and where Jesus is said to spend some of His time: 1) on the throne, sitting at the right hand of the Father, 2) interceding for the saints, and 3) building the New Jerusalem, the heavenly city. Of course, angelic beings, Old Testament believers, and New Testament Christians live in the third heaven as well.

told him, "You can't write any of it down." Why? Because God wants us to live by faith! . . . And, because He knew He was going to give us a glimpse of heaven in about 50 years, when He would have the apostle John write the Book of Revelation.

Now think back with me. The reason why I shared Paul's visit into heaven with you is because Paul said, "**God has not given us** (Christians) **the spirit of fear; but of power, and of love, and of a sound mind**." You see, while Paul may have been fearful of death before he saw heaven, it is clear that HE DIDN'T FEAR ANYTHING after he rose from being stoned (Acts 14:20). That's the reason why Paul was able to accomplish all that he did, while he was here. And that's the reason why Paul could say, "**For to me, to live *is* Christ, and to die *is* GAIN** (Philippians 1:21)!" That's the reason why Paul said, "**to be absent from the body** . . . is **to be present with the Lord** (2 Corinthians 5:8)!" That's why Paul said, "**I am in a strait betwixt two, having a desire to depart, and to be with Christ; which is FAR BETTER: nevertheless to abide in the flesh *is* more needful for you** (Philippians 1:23-24)."

God allowed Paul to see heaven. And after Paul saw heaven HE WASN'T AFRAID OF DEATH ANYMORE! It is on the basis of this FACT that a Christian can know for sure that heaven exists. Heaven is not simply some figment of our imagination. Heaven is not some pie in the sky, bye and bye fantasy. Heaven is a real place! And we can know that heaven is a real place, because Paul saw it!

JESUS PAID FOR OUR SINS

Now with this in mind, my first point is this. A Christian can be sure they will spend eternity in heaven, because Jesus Christ has paid the penalty for all our sins.

84

I want to take you back to that fateful day when the Lord Jesus Christ died on the cross, because I really want you to see what took place. Let's look at the 27ᵗʰ chapter of Matthew first. Matthew says in verses 45 and 46, "from noon until 3 o'clock **there was darkness over all the land**. And at about 3 o'clock **Jesus cried with a loud voice, saying, "Eli, Eli, lama sabachthani?" that is to say, "My God, My God, why hast Thou forsaken Me?"**

The first thing I want you to notice is that there was darkness over all the land. What's the significance of that? For a long time I didn't know. Then one day, as I was sitting in church, the Lord revealed to me that the darkness signified God's judgment. Did you know that almost every time darkness is mentioned in the Bible, someone or something has been judged, is being judged, or will be judged in the future? . . . The Bible says when Jesus Christ hung on the cross **there was darkness over all the land**. Who was being judged? Jesus! But not for any sins that He committed. He NEVER committed any sin. Jesus was being judged, because the Father had placed all the sins of mankind upon Him. That's why Jesus cried out, "**My God, My God, why hast Thou forsaken Me**?" Because during those three hours of darkness, God the Father, placed all the sins of the world on Christ!

The next thing I want you to notice is that the Lord Jesus cried out while there was darkness over all the land. In other words, Christ Jesus cried out while it was still dark! Do you understand the significance of that? Jesus is being judged for your sins and my sins, in DARKNESS! . . . During those three hours, while Jesus hung on the cross, He experienced the torment of hell and the lake of fire for every man, woman, boy, and girl. During those three hours He experienced an eternity of torment in hell and the lake of fire! Now, I can't explain that. There's no way I (a finite being) can explain the eternal nature of the judgment of Almighty God! But I know this. During those three hours of darkness, Jesus did what every unsaved person in hell does. He cried out in pain and anguish!

Do you remember how the Bible describes hell and the lake of fire? Hell is described as a place where the fire is never quenched (see Mark 9:42-48). The lake of fire is described as a place of outer darkness. As a furnace of fire in which the unsaved will be cast: where there shall be weeping, and wailing, and gnashing of teeth (see Matthew 13:49-50 and 22:13). . . . That's what Jesus experienced for all of us. He paid the penalty for all our sins, because He loves us.

And after the darkness was lifted, do you know what our Lord Jesus said? "**I thirst** (John 19:28)." Well yeah . . . I guess so. If you had just experienced an eternity in hell and the lake of fire you'd be thirsty too! Then shortly after this Jesus said, "**It is finished** (John 19:30)." What was finished? God's plan of salvation, for mankind, was now finished! The penalty for sin had now, once and for all, been paid in full! That's why 1 John 2:2 says, "**He** (Jesus Christ) **is the propitiation for our sins: and not for ours only, but also for *the sins of* the whole world!**" As the song says, "Jesus *truly* paid it all, all to Him I owe, sin had left a crimson stain, He washed it white as snow."[2]

So my first point is simply this. The first reason why I know a Christian can be sure they will spend eternity in heaven, is because the Lord Jesus Christ has paid the penalty for all our sins.

---

[2] Elvina M. Hall and John T. Grape, *Jesus Paid it All* (1865), the refrain.

WE HAVE THE RIGHTEOUSNESS OF CHRIST

My second point, my second reason why I know a Christian can be sure they will spend eternity in heaven is because they have the righteousness of Christ.

In 2 Corinthians 5:21 the apostle Paul wrote, **"For He has made Him *to be* sin for us, who knew no sin; that we might be made the righteousness of God in Him."** This is another truly significant verse of Scripture. When we examine this verse we discover that He (the Father) made Him (Jesus Christ) to be sin for us. God placed the sins of the world on Jesus – **who knew no sin**. In other words, our sins were placed in Christ's body. He was literally made sin for us, in order that **we might be made the righteousness of God in Him**. What does that mean? It means that when a person receives Jesus Christ as their personal Lord and Savior, a divine transaction takes place. The moment you receive Jesus Christ by faith, all your sins (past, present, and future) are placed in Christ's body; and all His righteousness is placed in your body. Thus, from God's point of view, from that moment on, you are as righteous as Christ! Once again, please notice, I didn't say from man's point of view – from our point of view. For we see ourselves as sinners saved by grace, because we still sin! But God sees us (Christians), as righteous. That's why He calls us "saints."

For example, when the apostle Paul wrote the church at Philippi do you know how he addressed them? He writes, ". . . **To all the saints in Christ Jesus which are at Philippi, with the bishops and deacons** (Philippians 1:1)." Did you know that, Biblically speaking, there are only two offices in the church? The first is Bishop (or Pastor), and the second is Deacon; and the rest of the congregation is simply known as SAINTS. The word saint comes from the Greek word "hagios." It means "holy ones," or "set-apart ones." You see, in the Church Age (the age or "dispensation" we are now living in), the Bible designates all Christians as "saints." Therefore, a Christian is not a saint because he does good works (which is what most people think). A Christian is a saint, because he has been made holy (positionally) by God, and set apart for His service.

I know some may not agree with this, but all you have to do is look at the 4th chapter of Philippians. In verses 2 and 3 Paul says, "**I beseech Euodias, and beseech Syntyche, that they be of the same mind in the Lord. And I intreat you also, true yokefellow, help those women which labored with me in the gospel.**" You know, sometimes, we get nostalgic and think, everybody in the first century church always got along with each other. They really loved one another. Why can't we be more like them? But the truth is, they were human beings with a sin nature too. Paul says these women were at odds with one another. They were holding a grudge against one another. And their lack of forgiveness was affecting the unity and effectiveness of the church. Thus Paul earnestly asked them to **be of the same mind**: to make things right, and forgive one another.

Now obviously, these two women were sinning against each other. Yet Paul called them, along with all the other members of the congregation, "saints!" Proving beyond a shadow of a doubt, that in this age, the Bible "designates" all Christians as saints!

The Lord calls us saints, because He sees us as being righteous. Romans 5:19 says, "**For as by one man's disobedience many were made sinners, so also by the obedience of one shall many be made righteous.**" When a person receives Jesus Christ as their personal Lord and Savior by faith, they are made (past tense) righteous. Romans 10:9-10 says, "**if thou shalt confess with your mouth the Lord Jesus,**

and shalt believe in your heart that God has raised Him from the dead, thou shalt be saved. For with the heart man believes unto righteousness (i.e., man believes resulting in righteousness)." We have been made righteous because a divine transaction occurred when Jesus Christ took away all our sins upon the cross.

Now I know this would never happen, because the Lord's angels always obey Him. They're not like us. They ALWAYS obey the Lord. But let's just suppose that a Christian dies. And he goes up to the third heaven to spend eternity with God. And as he gets closer and closer he hears music, and singing, and laughter. He even hears the voices of old friends who've gone on before him. But as he approaches the pearly gates, an angel stands in his way and blocks his path – and demands an answer to the question, "Why he should be allowed to enter into heaven?" Now again, this would never happen. But if it did, do you know how fast Jesus would get off His throne and rebuke that angel, and say, "Get out of his way, for he is righteous! He is holy, because I died for him! And the Father has adopted him! Therefore, this is his home! Get out of the way. Out of the way! . . ." And then Jesus would turn to that saint and say, "Come dear one, and enter into the joy of your Lord (see Galatians 4:1-7 and Matthew 25:21)."

You see, a Christian can know for sure that they will spend eternity in heaven, because they have received the righteousness of Christ.

MANY OLD TESTAMENT SAINTS ARE IN HEAVEN

The third reason why I know a Christian can be sure they will spend eternity in heaven is because some of the Old

Testament believers have already been resurrected and taken up into heaven.

Let's go back to the crucifixion of Christ. In the 27th chapter of his gospel, Matthew tells us they placed Jesus between two thieves. One was on the right, and the other was on the left. Now they were both guilty. They were criminals! But Jesus wasn't a criminal. As we've said before, He had done nothing wrong! Yet He was falsely accused by the religious leaders and sentenced to death. . . . So there they all are, each of them, hanging on a cross. And as the people passed by, they reviled Jesus. In other words, they mocked Him, they taunted Him, they blasphemed Him – they wagged their heads in disgust at Him, saying, **"If You are the Son of God, come down from the cross** (see Matthew 27:38-40)."

The people mocked Him. The religious leaders mocked Him. The Roman soldiers mocked Him. And strange as it may seem, the two thieves mocked Him. . . . "So you're the King of Israel? I didn't know I was in the presence of royalty! . . . Hey King, why don't you use some of your divine influence and power and get us off of these crosses (see Matthew 27:41-44 and Luke 23:35-37)."

You talk about a display of human depravity! Of human folly! This is the true nature of man. To kick the righteous, sinless, Son of God, when He's down! That's why the Bible says, **the carnal mind *is* enmity** (i.e., at war) **against God** (Romans 8:7). Jeremiah said, the human heart (yours and mine included), ***is* deceitful above all *things* . . . and desperately wicked** (Jeremiah 17:9)! I mean think about it. In the last few hours of their lives, all these thieves could find time to do was curse, mock, ridicule, and blaspheme Jesus, the Lamb of God.

But after a while one of them came to his senses. He turned to the other criminal and said, "Don't you fear God (see Luke 23:39-41)?" He realized, FINALLY, that he was guilty, and his punishment was just. He saw himself as a sinner, and he made no more excuses. He acknowledged his guilt, and passed judgment upon himself. Every sinner must do this, before he, or she, can be reconciled to God. We must see ourselves as lost . . . totally and completely lost! And then we must repent and place our faith in Christ.

We must have faith, genuine faith: the kind of faith that transcends common sense. We must believe with all our heart, that Jesus will forgive our sins, save us, and give us eternal life. Think about this dying thief. How did he have faith to believe in a man who was in the same predicament as himself? Jesus didn't perform any miracles in front of him. Jesus was weak, He was disgraced! His enemies had seemingly triumphed over Him! His friends had forsaken Him! And public opinion was unanimously against Him! . . . Yet, despite all these circumstances which were surrounding him, he saw the Savior! He saw the King of kings and Lord of lords! You ask, "How could this be?" Simple! He had faith. Genuine faith!!! So he turned to Jesus and said, "**Lord, remember me when You come into Your kingdom** (see Luke 23:42)." He asked Jesus to save him. He said, "Lord, when You set up Your Kingdom in the by and by, in that great Gettin' Up morning, remember me!"

Now at this point, Jesus could have said a lot of things. He could have said, "You dirty rotten no good sinner. You're not worthy to enter into My kingdom." He could have said, "You mocked Me! And now you expect Me to save you! Forget it!" But He said, "**Today, thou shalt be with Me in paradise** (Luke 23:43)."

Now notice, not in the hereafter, not in the by and by, not two thousand years from now, but today! What did Jesus mean? Well first of all, He meant literally, that day, he would be with Him in paradise. But what you must understand is that in the Old Testament days, paradise was not in heaven. Paradise was in the heart of the earth!

A few words of clarification might be helpful at this point:

Most people believe that the New Testament begins when you come to the 1st chapter of the Book of Matthew. But the Book of Hebrews clearly states, the New Testament didn't begin until **the death of the testator** (Hebrews 9:16-17). That means the New Testament didn't begin until the death of Christ. Now, since Jesus is talking to the thief on the cross that obviously means He's still alive: which obviously means, we're still in the Old Testament. You see the New Testament doesn't begin until Matthew 27:50, until Mark 15:37, until Luke 23:46, until John 19:30.

Now, as I said a few moments ago, you must understand that during the Old Testament days, paradise was not in heaven, it was in the heart of the earth. The reason why is because the Old Testament believer's sins were never "truly" taken away until Christ died. Think back with me. Do you remember what God commanded the Old Testament believers to do when they sinned? He commanded them to bring an unblemished animal to the temple, to be sacrificed in their stead. Thus, day after day, the people brought their animals to be sacrificed in the temple. But those animal sacrifices only covered their sins (see Psalm 32:1). They didn't take them away. . . . Hebrews 10:4 clearly states, "*it is* **impossible for *the* blood of bulls and of goats to take away sins**." Therefore, since an Old Testament believer's sins weren't "truly" taken away, they couldn't go "up" into heaven. Therefore, when they died they went to paradise, which at that time, was in the heart of the earth.

THE BIBLICAL VIEW OF HELL

At this point, we need to take a brief theological detour and talk about hell. Now, don't tune me out. Don't switch the channel. I promise, in a few moments, it will become clear to you why we need to do this.

In Ezekiel 31:15-18 the Bible says, **"Thus says the Lord God; In the day when he went down to the grave I caused a mourning: I covered the deep over him, and I restrained the floods thereof, and the great waters were stayed: and I caused Lebanon to mourn for him, and all the trees of the field fainted because of him. I made the nations to shake at the sound of his fall, when I cast him down to hell with them that descend into the pit: and all the trees of Eden, the choice and best of Lebanon, all that drink water, shall be comforted in the nether parts of the earth. They also went down into hell with him unto** *them that be* **slain with the sword; and** *they that were* **his arm,** *that* **dwelt under his shadow in the midst of the heathen. To whom art thou thus like in glory and in greatness among the trees of Eden? yet thou shalt be brought down with the trees of Eden unto the nether parts of the earth: thou shalt lie in the midst of the uncircumcised, with** *them that be* **slain by the sword. This** *is* **Pharaoh and all his multitude, says the Lord God."**

This is a very unusual passage of Scripture. In these verses Ezekiel is comparing wicked nations and their rulers to trees. And he says these wicked people not only **went down to the grave**, but God cast them **down to hell**. Now, what I want you to notice, is that the Bible says hell is **in the nether parts of the earth**. Hell is right beneath your feet – in the heart of the earth.

The next thing I want you to see is that hell is divided up into 4 compartments. Now for our purposes, and in order to save time, I want to talk about three of them.[3] The first is called Tartarus.

2 Peter 2:4 says, ". . . **God did not spare the** demons **that sinned, but cast *them* down to hell, and delivered *them* into chains of darkness, to be reserved unto judgment**." Every time the word hell is used in the New Testament, it is translated from either the Greek word "hades" or "geenna." That is, every time except for here. The Greek word which is translated "hell" in this verse is literally "Tartarus." This is the only time in Scripture this word is used. Tartarus is a place, located in hell, where God has already cast some demons. You see, they acted so wickedly in the days of Noah that God had to judge them, and send them to hell early.

The second place (or compartment) in hell is what we normally think of when we talk about hell. It is a place of "torments." This is the place where God sends the unsaved when they die. And the third place is called "Abraham's Bosom" (or paradise). This is where God sent the Old Testament saints when they died.

---

[3] The fourth place (or compartment) in hell is called Death. Rev. 20:13-14 says, "and death and hell delivered up the dead which were in them: and they were judged, every one according to their works. And death and hell were cast into the lake of fire. This is the second death." The basic order of prophetic events is: 1) the Rapture, 2) the Tribulation Period, 3) the Battle of Armageddon, and 4) the Millennial Kingdom Age of Christ. In the Millennial Kingdom all Christians and tribulation saints will have glorified bodies. But the people who survive the Tribulation Period will remain in their natural physical bodies. Thus, those who become believers in the Millennial Kingdom will go to this place called Death when they die.

Torments and Abraham's Bosom are both mentioned in Luke 16:19-31. Luke says, **"There was a certain rich man, which was clothed in purple and fine linen, and fared sumptuously every day; and there was a certain beggar named Lazarus, which was laid at his gate, full of sores, and desiring to be fed with the crumbs which fell from the rich man's table: moreover the dogs came and licked his sores. And it came to pass, that the beggar died, and was carried by the angels into Abraham's bosom; the rich man also died, and was buried: and in hell he lifted up his eyes, being in torments;** *and* **he sees Abraham afar off, and Lazarus in his bosom. And he cried and said, Father Abraham, have mercy on me, and send Lazarus, that he may dip the tip of his finger in water, and cool my tongue; for I am tormented in this flame. But Abraham said, Son, remember that you in your lifetime received your good things, and likewise Lazarus evil things: but now he is comforted, and you are tormented. And beside all this, between us and you there is a great gulf fixed: so that they which would pass from this place to you cannot; neither can they pass to us, that** *would come* **from that place. Then he said, I pray thee therefore, father, that you** would **send him to my father's house: for I have five brothers; that he may testify unto them, lest they also come into this place of torment. Abraham said to him, They have Moses and the prophets; let them hear them. And he said, Nay, father Abraham: but if one went unto them from the dead, they will repent. And he said to him, If they will not hear Moses and the prophets, neither will they be persuaded, though one rose from the dead."**

Now, Luke says Lazarus went to Abraham's Bosom (paradise). But the rich man went to hell (or literally, the "torments" portion of hell). Why did Lazarus go to Abraham's Bosom? Well, first of all, God bestowed His grace upon him. Second, he performed the Old Testament sacrifices. And third, by faith, he believed that God would one day send the Savior who would not merely cover his sins, but take his sins away. (This was the Plan of Salvation in the Old Testament "Dispensation of The Law!")

Why did the rich man go to the "torments" part of hell? Well, God bestowed His grace upon him, just like He did with Lazarus. But, he didn't perform the Old Testament sacrifices. And he didn't believe God would send the Savior. Or he didn't care. He didn't have faith! . . . He didn't need faith. His faith was in his riches. So he went to the "torments" part of hell.

Now, to make sure you understand this, please listen to verses 23-26 again. Luke says, "**and in hell he lifted up his eyes, being in torments;** *and* **he saw Abraham afar off, and Lazarus in his bosom. And he cried and said, Father Abraham, have mercy on me, and send Lazarus, that he may dip the tip of his finger in water, and cool my tongue; for I am tormented in this flame. But Abraham said, Son, remember that you in your lifetime received your good things, and likewise Lazarus evil things: but now he is comforted, and you are tormented. And beside all this, between us and you there is a great gulf fixed: so that they which would pass from this place to you cannot; neither can they pass to us, that** *would come* **from that place.**"

Were you listening? The Bible says they could SEE one another. In other words, they were in the same place! They were BOTH in hell! One was in "torments," and the other was in "Abraham's Bosom." And just to make sure that you understood both places were different, even though they were in the same location, the Bible says in verse 25, that Lazarus was now "comforted." Comforted! That's a word filled with meaning. It comes from the Greek word "parakaleo." And it means to ease, and eliminate the grief of . . . to console . . . to give relief to; it means to give hope to, and to cause to rejoice; to utter a SHOUT of triumph! . . . When Lazarus died he went to Abraham's Bosom, and he rejoiced, because ALL OF HIS TROUBLES were OVER!!! He was in paradise!

So when the Old Testament believers died, they went to Abraham's Bosom, because the Old Testament sacrifices couldn't take away their sins. Only Jesus Christ, the Lamb of God, the Savior, can take away sins.

BACK TO THE CROSS

So when Jesus looked at the thief on the cross and said, **"Today, thou shalt be with Me in paradise**," He literally meant TODAY, you shall be with Me in paradise (in Abraham's Bosom), with all the other Old Testament saints.

Make no mistake about it, when a person dies, they don't stay in the grave until eternity begins. No! The body stays in the grave. But the person's soul and spirit either goes to paradise, or to torments.

THE FIRST CHRISTIAN

Jesus died about four hours after He spoke to the thief. When He died, His soul and spirit went to hell.

Now please understand, when Jesus went to hell, He didn't go there to suffer any punishment. Nor did He go there to be tormented in any flames! Remember, He experienced that pain and anguish (the penalty for sin) while He was hanging on the cross, during those three hours of darkness!

About an hour after Jesus died, both thieves died. And when they died their souls and spirits went to hell too. Of course, one went to "Abraham's Bosom," and the other went to "torments."

But do you know what's truly significant? The thief that went to Abraham's Bosom died, AFTER Jesus yielded up His spirit. That means he died after **the death of the testator.** Do you know what that means? That means THAT THIEF was the first person to place his faith in Jesus Christ, and then die in the New Testament! And since he believed in faith – and faith alone, apart from works – he became the first Christian![4]

WHAT DID JESUS DO?

Now, the next question that we must deal with is this. "What did Jesus do while He was in hell?" Did He take a brief vacation? Did He just twiddle His thumbs, for three days and three nights? . . . Do the Scriptures shed any light on what He did? . . . Of course they do.

What was the first thing Jesus did when He went down into hell? He got the keys of hell and death. Revelation 1:17-18 says, "**. . . I am the first and the last:** *I am* **He that lives, and was dead; and, behold, I am alive forevermore, Amen; and have the keys of hell and of death.**"

Some believe our Lord Jesus has always had these keys. But I believe He had to earn the right to get them by dying on

---

[4] Even if you are on your deathbed, you can still ask Jesus to be your Lord and Savior, and ask Him to save you, just like the dying thief did. Remember, God loves you! It is Satan that hates you; and he wants you to burn in the lake of fire with him, for all of eternity. Don't let Satan deceive or trick you into thinking it's too late. Receive the Lord Jesus Christ by faith right now.

the cross for our sins. . . . Some believe Jesus had to wrestle these keys out of Satan's hand. But I don't believe that, because Satan doesn't have control over what goes on in hell. Nor does he have the authority to cast people into hell. Only God has the authority to do that. . . . Some believe these keys are figurative. But I tend to believe that they are literal keys, because both death and hell have gates (see Job 38:16-17 and Matthew 16:18).[5]

The second thing Jesus did when He went to hell was preach to the spirits in prison. 1 Peter 3:18-19 says, **"For Christ also has suffered once for sins, *the* just for *the* unjust, that He might bring us to God, being put to death in the flesh, but quickened by the Spirit: by which also He went and preached unto the spirits in prison."**

The apostle Peter says, "Jesus preached to the spirits (i.e., the unsaved, and the demons) in hell." Now at first glance, it appears that Jesus is giving these people and demons a second chance to receive Him as their Lord and Savior. But that's not what the word "preached" means in these verses. This word "preached," comes from the Greek word "ekeruxen." It means to announce, or, to proclaim. Thus, when Jesus spoke, He did not preach the gospel to them. He proclaimed to them that they had made the wrong choice in life: that they should have accepted Him as their Lord and Savior; that they should have obeyed Him, rather than Satan. Thus, He proclaimed their doom! Jesus (probably with tears in His eyes) told them,

---

[5] Now I know we always interpret Matthew 16:18 as, ". . . the *powers* of hell shall not prevail against the church." And practically speaking, this is true. But there is a literal aspect to these gates. The reason why the gates of hell shall not prevail against the church (i.e., Christians) is because when we die, our soul and spirit will not go down into Abraham's bosom, in the heart of the earth. Our soul and spirit will go up into heaven, to be with the Lord Jesus Christ.

because you chose not to accept Me, you will spend all eternity in the lake of fire!

After Jesus preached to the spirits in prison, He took the keys of death and hell, and opened the gate to Abraham's Bosom; and freed many of the Old Testament saints! And, the thief! Matthew 27:50-53 says, **"Jesus, when He had cried again with a loud voice, yielded up *His* spirit. And, behold, the veil of the temple was rent in two from the top to the bottom; and the earth did quake, and the rocks rent; and the graves were opened; and many bodies of the saints which slept arose, and came out of the graves after His resurrection, and went into the holy city, and appeared unto many."**

Every time I ponder these verses I experience a sense of awe. In the last few moments of Jesus' life the Scriptures say He cried again with a loud voice. John 19:30 tells us He cried out, **"It is finished!"** Which was not a cry of anguish; it was the shout of a man who had just won the victory! **"IT IS FINISHED!"** What was finished? God's plan of salvation, which would save all who trusted in Christ by faith! Then after Jesus cried, **"It is finished,"** Luke 23:46 tells us He said, **"Father, into Thy hands I commend My spirit."** And then He **yielded up *His* spirit.**

Now, pay very close attention to what Matthew writes. Matthew says, "After Jesus died, there was a great earthquake, and many of the Old Testament believers **graves were opened**.[6]

---

[6] Please note, Matthew doesn't say "all" the Old Testament saints came out of the graves. He says "many." The reason why is because when Peter preached the gospel on the day of Pentecost, he told the people that king David was still in the grave (Acts 2:22-36). Thus, God has only resurrected those Old Testament saints who lived from the time of Adam to the time the law was given by Moses. Now why has God done this? The reason why is because He has promised the rest of the Old Testament believers that

And, when Jesus rose from the dead, THEY ROSE FROM THE DEAD TOO! **And went into** Jerusalem, **and appeared unto many!**" In other words, very early on Sunday morning, Jesus was resurrected, and, these Old Testament believers, who had been in Abraham's bosom, were resurrected too! . . . But not only that, the thief, who had also been in Abraham's bosom WAS RESURRECTED TOO!

That's incredible! But Matthew doesn't stop there. He says they went into Jerusalem! Can you imagine eating an early morning snack in a café? And as you finish your wine, you see Shem walk through the wall stating, "Those that were captive have now been delivered!" Can you imagine being a guard, on patrol at the temple, keeping the peace? And as you turn around you see Rachel, shining as a star saying, "The Lamb of God has taken away my sins!" Can you imagine getting up to use the bathroom? And as you look out your bedroom window you see Eliezer, floating by, and shouting, "This mortal has put on immortality!" Can you imagine the thief, who had just been on the cross three days earlier, going back to his family

---

they would be resurrected in their natural, physical bodies: so that they could experience the blessings of the Millennial Kingdom. You see, God promised Abraham that He would give his descendants the land of Israel: all the land that He showed him in a vision (see Gen. 12:1-7, Gen. 13:14-17, and Gen. 15:1-21). However, to this day, Israel has never received all the land that God promised Abraham. So even though this may sound a little strange to us, when Jesus comes back to rule and reign for 1,000 years, He will resurrect these Old Testament saints in their natural, physical bodies, just like He resurrected Lazarus (John 11:1-45). And God will do this so that they will be able to experience the blessings He promised Abraham (see Ezek. 37:1-28, Isa. 26:19, Isa. 60:1-22, Isa. 35:1-7, and Isa. 11:1-10). You see, God always keeps His promises. Of course, since these saints are raised in their natural bodies, they will die again. (In other words, they won't receive immortal bodies, like the Jewish tribulation saints in Dan. 12:1-2, until after the Millennial Kingdom Age is over.) However, when the 1,000 year reign is over, they will be resurrected and given immortal bodies (see Rev. 20:11-15).

and telling them, "Jesus Christ is the Savior? He really is the Savior! Believe in Him, and receive Him!" The Old Testament saints and the thief spent the early morning hours in Jerusalem. But as the sun began to rise, Jesus took them up into heaven.

We know this, because Paul tells us, "**When He ascended up on high, He led captivity captive, and gave gifts to men. Now that** *expression*, **'He ascended,'** what does it mean? Obviously, **that He also descended first into the lower parts of the earth? And He that descended is the same also that ascended up far above all heavens, that He might fill all things** (see Ephesians 4:8-10)." Now obviously, this is not the same ascension that took place in Acts 1:6-11. This ascension took place early on Easter morning. But since most people don't truly know what happened that morning, they don't realize that the Old Testament saints and the thief (the first Christian) were taken up into heaven by Christ.

Please look at verse 8 again. Do you see that phrase, "**He led captivity captive**?" It's really a military term. It depicts the triumphal return of a king from battle, who displays "as the spoils of victory," the captives that were once imprisoned by the enemy. Thus, in His crucifixion and resurrection, Jesus defeated sin and death! And since these enemies were totally and completely conquered (they can never again mount a counter attack), He led a whole host of captives from Abraham's Bosom, right on up into heaven! Of course, after He took them up to heaven, He came back down to earth and showed His followers, and His disciples, that He had indeed risen from the grave.

So, how can a Christian know for sure, that they will spend eternity in heaven when they die? Well, based on what the Word of God says:

1. A Christian can be sure that they will spend eternity in heaven, because Jesus Christ has paid the penalty for all their sins.

2. A Christian can be sure that they will spend eternity in heaven, because they have received the righteousness of Christ.

3. A Christian can be sure that they will spend eternity in heaven, because some of the Old Testament believers (as an example and encouragement to us) have already been resurrected, and taken up into heaven.

JESUS WILL NEVER LEAVE US

The fourth, and final reason why I know a Christian can be sure that they will spend eternity in heaven is because Jesus Christ has promised, He will never leave us.

Jesus says in Hebrews 13:5, "**I will never leave you, nor forsake you**." Now this is a very simple verse. And yet, its meaning is quite profound. I mean just think about it for a minute. Jesus says, "**I will never leave you**." Where is Jesus? Well, based on Revelation 3:20, He's inside of us. He's inside of "Christians."

This again is another major difference between the Old Testament and the New Testament. In the Old Testament, the Spirit of the Lord (the Holy Spirit) "came upon," or "entered into" believers at different times, but He was never obligated to "remain," or "stay" in them (see Judges 14:5-6 and 15:14, and, Ezekiel 2:1-2 and 3:24). Thus, when an Old Testament believer sinned, the Holy Spirit would almost always leave them. In the New Testament however, the Bible clearly states that the Holy Spirit "resides" or "lives" in the Christian forever (see John 14:16-17 and 1 Corinthians 6:19-20). And, it also states that Jesus Christ "resides" in us as well (see John 14:20 and 14:23). Wow! Did you catch that? Can you grasp what I just said? If you're a Christian, both the Holy Spirit and Jesus Christ live inside of you. God lives, inside of you! That's why 1 Corinthians 6:19 says, "Our bodies are the temple of God."

Now, if Jesus lives inside of you, and He promises never to leave you, how can you lose your salvation or go to hell (i.e., the "Torments" portion of hell)? If you're a "Christian," and you were to go to hell, that would only mean one of two things. Either Jesus left you, which would make Him a liar. Or, Jesus was cast into hell with you, and will spend all of eternity with you, in the flames of the lake of fire – which would be absurd! . . . Take your pick.

Remember, Jesus said, "**My God, My God, why hast Thou forsaken Me**?" while He was experiencing the torment of Hell and the Lake of Fire. And He said, "**I thirst**" after the three hours of darkness were over. And why did Jesus die on the cross? To pay the penalty for our sins! Now, let's get specific. How many sins did Jesus actually pay for? Well, 1 John 2:2 says, "**He** (Jesus Christ) **is the propitiation** (the atoning sacrifice) **for our sins: and not for ours only, but also for *the sins of* the whole world**." How many sins did Jesus pay for? He paid for all the sins that would ever be committed. Not just the sins of all Christians. He paid for the sins of every person who would ever live! And when did He do that? Over 2,000 years ago!

Now think with me, realistically and honestly. Before you were born didn't God know how many sins you would commit in your lifetime? . . . I mean He's God. He knows everything, right? And before you were born, didn't Jesus pay for your sins? Well, if Jesus paid for your sins over 2,000 years ago, that must mean He's PAID for all the sins you've committed in the past . . . He's PAID for all the sins you will commit today . . . and, He's already PAID for all the sins you will commit in the future!!! . . . RIGHT?

Well if that's the case, what sin could you possibly commit that Jesus hasn't already paid for? Do you see my point? If you're a Christian, all your sins, past, present, and future have already been paid for by the Lord Jesus Christ! . . . Therefore, if you were to die, and go to hell, that would mean that Jesus didn't pay for ALL your sins . . . which would make God's Word a lie . . . which would mean that Jesus would have to spend all of eternity, in torment, inside of you, because He didn't pay for ALL your sins – because Jesus said, "**I will never leave you, nor forsake you.**" Do you see how ridiculous that sounds? And yet, some Christians actually believe they can lose their salvation and go to hell when they die.

Now, I know some of you may be thinking, "Sure, Jesus would never leave us, but we might leave Him!" Oh yeah? How are you going to leave someone who lives inside of you? Come on, that's just like saying you're going to leave your nervous system. Can you take your nervous system out of your body? No! Even doctors can't operate on you and take it out. Now, if you can't do a simple little thing like leave your own nervous system, how are you going to leave Christ, which is at least a trillion times more difficult?

But someone who may still not be convinced might say, "I can leave Jesus by sinning!" Oh really? Show me that verse in the Bible. Show me a verse that says, if a Christian commits some sin, that sin will cause them to leave Jesus. No such verse exists in the Bible, because Jesus said, "**I will never leave you, nor forsake you.**" Jesus Christ will NEVER leave us.

Now, you might find a verse that says God will leave a Tribulation believer. You might even find a verse that says Jesus will leave a believer during the Millennial Kingdom Age. But you will never find a verse that says Jesus will leave a Christian in the Church Age, because Jesus has paid the penalty for all **our sins** (past, present, and future) and because the Bible says Jesus paid the penalty for our sins **once for all!** In other words, once for all time!

Listen to what the author of Hebrews says . . .

For the law, having a shadow of good things to come, *and* not the very image of the things, can never, with those sacrifices . . . make the comers to the altar **perfect. For then, would they not have ceased to be offered? because the worshipers, once purged, would have had no more conscience of sins. But in those *sacrifices there is* a remembrance, *made* again, of sins every year. *For it is* impossible for *the* blood of bulls and of goats to take away sins.** Therefore, **He says, Sacrifice and offering Thou didst not desire, but a body hast Thou prepared Me:** for **in burnt offerings and *sacrifices* for sin Thou hast had no pleasure. Then He** (Jesus) **said, Lo, I come to do Thy will, O God.** Thus, **He** took **away the first** covenant (i.e., the Old Testament), **that He may establish the second.** Therefore **by *His* will, we are sanctified through the offering of the body of Jesus Christ once *for all*** (see Hebrews 10:1-10).

And every priest stands daily ministering and offering oftentimes the same sacrifices, which can never take away sins: but this Man (Jesus), **after He had offered one sacrifice for sins forever, sat down at the right hand of God. . . . For by one offering He**

has perfected forever them that are sanctified. And
the Holy Spirit also is a witness to us: for He had
said before, **this** *is* **the covenant that I will make with
them after those days, says the Lord; I will put my
laws into their hearts, and in their minds I will write
them; and their sins and iniquities I will remember
no more.** Now where remission (or forgiveness) **of
these** *is,* *there is* **no more** need to make an **offering for
sin** (see Hebrews 10:11-18).

And since there is no longer any need to make an offering
for sin, there is no sin that you could commit that would cause
Jesus to leave you.

Therefore, a Christian, can know for sure, that they will
spend eternity in heaven because, Jesus Christ has paid
the penalty for all our sins; because we have received the
righteousness of Christ; because many of the Old Testament
believers have already been taken up into heaven; and because
Jesus has promised, **I will never leave you, nor forsake you.**

WE WILL SPEND ETERNITY IN HEAVEN

There is one ultimate, inevitable, reality. Unless we are here
when the rapture takes place, we will all die. But a Christian
can take comfort in knowing that when he or she dies, they
will spend eternity in heaven. . . . Now when I say "comfort,"
I'm not talking about some sort of mumbo jumbo that we can
psychologically use, to sooth our fears, when that inevitable
day comes. No! I'm talking about real comfort, because when a
Christian dies they will immediately be carried up into heaven.

Therefore, the Bible encourages us to **walk by faith**, and **not
by sight** (2 Corinthians 5:7). But a Christian doesn't simply put

blind faith in the Scriptures. Our faith is based upon historical fact. When the apostle Paul was stoned, he went to heaven! He was there! But it wasn't his time to die yet. God still had more work for him to do. So the Lord sent him back down to earth. . . . When Paul came back down here (and believe me, he would have rather stayed in heaven) he said, "Even though I can't tell you what I saw, or what I heard, I want you to know I WAS ACTUALLY THERE!" That's why Paul says, "**to be absent from the body**, is **to be present with the Lord**" (see Philippians 1:21-24 and 2 Corinthians 5:8).

Let me close with three final passages of Scripture:

The Book of Romans says, "**And we know that all things** (even death) **work together for good to them that love God, to them who are the called according to *His* purpose. For whom He did foreknow, He also did predestinate to be conformed to the image of His Son, that He might be the firstborn among many brethren. Moreover whom He did predestinate, them He also called: and whom He called, them He also justified: and whom He justified, them He also glorified!** . . . **What shall we then say to these things? If God *be* for us, who *can be* against us?** If the Father **spared not His own Son, but delivered Him up for us all, how shall He not with Him, also freely give us all things? Who shall lay any** charge against **God's elect? It is God that justifies.** Who shall condemn us? (No one!) For **it is Christ that died, yea rather, that is risen again; who**, even now, is **at the right hand of God**, making **intercession for us.**" (see Romans 8:28-34).

Therefore, we have nothing to fear.

Jesus said, "**Let not your heart be troubled: ye believe in God, believe also in Me. In My Father's house are many mansions: if** *it were* **not** *so,* **I would have told you. I go to prepare a place for you. And if I go and prepare a place for you, I will come again, and receive you unto Myself; that where I am,** *there* **ye may be also**" (see John 14:1-3).

Thus, when we go home, to be with the Lord . . . "**God shall wipe away all tears from** our **eyes; and there shall be no more death, neither sorrow, nor crying, neither shall there be any more pain: for the former things** shall be **passed away**" (see Revelation 21:4)!

Now just dwell on that. Don't let your mind wander or get distracted, or change the subject. Don't let the cares of this world force you to move on, to "so called" more important things! Someday, in the future, praise God, we shall be in heaven with our Lord and Savior Jesus Christ. And someday, He shall change (i.e., transform) our vile, sinful, aging, and decaying bodies! . . . Someday our bodies will be fashioned just like His glorious resurrection body! In other words, our bodies will be sinless, and holy! And we will never get sick or grow old again. We will never experience pain, broken bones, disease, or death again! We will never need glasses, or hearing aids, or dentures, or wigs again! And our new bodies will never need to be replenished by food or drink, or even sleep again. We will be visible and tangible: we will have flesh and bones. And yet, we will be able to walk through walls, and travel at the speed of thought. . . . And we will be recognizable: we will know all the saints, and all the saints will know us. And we will live in a mansion, in the New Jerusalem. Now just think about that! Take comfort in that, and be encouraged! . . . Rest in that!

Someday we will gather around the throne of Almighty God and sing praises to Him, and worship Him! And serve Him. And rule and reign with Him! We will be His kings, and priests! And we will experience love, joy, peace, and contentment. And most important of all, we will experience unending fellowship with all the saints, and with all the angelic beings, and, with the Father, the Son, and the Holy Spirit – for all eternity.

Bibliography

In the preparation of this book I have read several books and commentaries, and, listened to many cassette tapes and MP3s. While I am indebted to all those who have come before me, and appreciate their efforts to put down in writing or another medium what they have learned from their own study of the Scriptures, I do want to make it clear I do not necessarily agree with every interpretation, or theological position, that is presented by the authors below:

BOOKS

Bright, Bill. **How to Be Sure You Are a Christian.** Orlando, Fl.: New Life 2000 Publications, 1971.

Hartill, Edwin J. **Principles of Biblical Hermeneutics.** Grand Rapids, Mi.: Zondervan Publishing House, 1947.

LaHaye, Tim. **Spirit-Controlled Temperament.** Wheaton, Il.: Tyndale House Publishers, 1977.

McDowell, Josh. **Evidence That Demands a Verdict.** San Bernardino, Ca.: Here's Life Publishers, Inc., 1972.

McDowell, Josh. **Understanding Non-Christian Religions.** San Bernardino, Ca.: Here's Life Publishers, Inc., 1982.

Morison, Frank. **Who Moved The Stone?** London: Faber and Faber, 1958.

Pentecost, Dwight J. **Things Which Become Sound Doctrine.** Grand Rapids, Mi.: Zondervan Corporation, 1970.

Ridenour, Fritz. **So What's the Difference?** Ventura, Ca.: Regal Books, 1979.

Ruckman, Peter S. **How to Teach Dispensational Truth.** Pensacola, Fl.: Bible Believers Press, 1992.

Ryrie, Charles C. **Dispensationalism.** Chicago, Il.: Moody Press, 1995.

Swindoll, Charles R. **Eternal Security.** Portland, Or.: Multnomah Press, 1981.

Telchin, Stan. **Betrayed!** Old Tappen, NJ: Chosen Books, 1981.

Thomas, W. H. Griffith. **Christianity is Christ.** London: Church Book Room Press, 1909.

COMMENTARIES

Barclay, William. **The Letters to the Corinthians.** Philadelphia, Pa.: The Westminster Press, 1975.

Blackwood, Andrew W. **Ezekiel, Prophecy of Hope.** Grand Rapids, Mi.: Baker Book House, 1965.

Block, Daniel I. **The New International Commentary on the Old Testament, The Book of Ezekiel.** Grand Rapids, Mi.: Wm. B. Eerdmans Publishing Co., 1998.

Boice, James M. **The Gospel of John, Vol. 1-5.** Grand Rapids, Mi.: Zondervan Corp., 1985.

Brown, Raymond. **The Bible Speaks Today, The Message of Hebrews.** Downers Grove, Il.: Inter-Varsity Press, 1982.

Bruce, F. F. **The New International Commentary on the New Testament, The Book of the Acts.** Grand Rapids, Mi.: Wm. B. Eerdmans Publishing Co., 1984.

Burdick, Donald W. **The Expositors Bible Commentary, James, Vol. 12.** Grand Rapids, Mi.: Zondervan Publishing House, 1981.

Burdick, Donald W. **Everyman's Bible Commentary, The Epistles of John.** Chicago, Il.: Moody Press, 1970.

Cohen, Gary G. and Kirban, Salem. **Revelation Visualized.** Huntingdon, Pa.: Salem Kirban, Inc., 1971.

Criswell, W. A. **Isaiah an Exposition.** Grand Rapids, Mi.: Zondervan Publishing House, 1977.

DeHaan, M.R. **Studies in First Corithians.** Grand Rapids, Mi.: Lamplighter Books, 1966.

Erdman, Charles R. **The Epistle of Paul to the Philippians,** Philadelphia, Pa.: The Westminster Press, 1932.

Fee, Gordon. **The New International Commentary on the New Testament, The First Epistle to the Corinthians.** Grand Rapids, Mi.: Wm. B. Eerdmans Publishing Co., 1971.

Feinberg, Charles L. **The Prophecy of Ezekiel, The Glory of the Lord.** Chcago, Il.: Moody Press, 1969.

Greene, Oliver B. **The Second Epistle of Paul the Apostle to the Corinthians.** Greenville, SC.: The Gospel Hour, 1976.

Hiebert, Edmond D. **First Peter.** Chicago, Il.: Moody Press, 1984.

Hiebert, Edmond D. **Second Peter and Jude, An Expositional Commentary.** Greenville, SC.: Unusual Publications, 1989.

Hiebert, D. Edmond. **The Thessalonian Epistles, A call to Readiness.** Chicago, Il.: Moody Press, 1971.

Hughes Philip E. **The New International Commentary on the New Testament, The Second Epistle to the Corinthians.** Grand Rapids, Mi.: Wm. B. Eerdmans Publishing Co., 1962.

Laurin, Roy L. **2 Corinthians, Where Life Endures.** Grand Rapids, Mi.: Kregel Publications, 1985.

MacArthur, John. **A Bible Commentary for Laymen, Galatians, Liberated for Life.** Ventura, Ca.: Regal Books, 1975.

MacArthur, John. **The MacArthur New Testament Commentary, Ephesians.** Chicago, Il.: Moody Press, 1986.

MacArthur, John. **The MacArthur New Testament Commentary, Matthew, Vol. 1-4.** Chicago, Il.: Moody Press, 1989.

MacArthur, John. **The MacArthur New Testament Commentary, Acts, Vol. 2.** Chicago, Il.: Moody Press, 1996.

MacArthur, John. **The MacArthur New Testament Commentary, Hebrews.** Chicago, Il.: Moody Press, 1983.

McGee, J Vernon. **Thru the Bible, 1 Corinthians through Revelation.** Nashville, Tn.: Thomas Nelson Publishers, 1983.

Morris, Leon. **The New International Commentary on the New Testament, The Gospel of John.** Grand Rapids, Mi.: Wm. B. Eerdmans Publishing Co., 1971.

Patterson, Paige. **An Exposition of First Corinthians, The Troubled Triumphant Church.** Nashville, Tn.: Thomas Nelson Publishers, 1983.

Phillips, John. **Exploring Acts.** Neptune, NJ: Loizeaux Brothers, 1991.

Pink, Arthur W. **Exposition of the Gospel of John, Vol. 1-3.** Grand Rapids, Mi.: Zondervan Publishing House, 1975.

Pink, Arthur W. **An Exposition of Hebrews.** Grand Rapids, Mi.: Baker Book House, 1954. Publishing House, 1975.

Ruckman, Peter S. **The Bible Believer's Commentary Series, The Book of Matthew.** Pensacola, Fl.: Pensacola Bible Institute, 1970.

Ruckman, Peter S. **The Bible Believer's Commentary Series, The Books of First and Second Corinthians.** Pensacola, Fl.: Pensacola Bible Institute, 2002.

Ruckman, Peter S. **The Bible Believer's Commentary Series, The Books of the General Epistles, Vol. 2.** Pensacola, Fl.: Pensacola Bible Institute, 2004.

Ruckman, Peter S. **The Bible Believer's Commentary Series, The Book of Revelation.** Pensacola, Fl.: Pensacola Bible Institute, 1970.

Walvoord, John F. **The Revelation of Jesus Christ.** Chicago, Il.: Moody Press, 1966.

Walvoord, John F. **Bible Study Commentary, The Thessalonian Epistles.** Grand Rapids, Mi.: Zondervan Publishing House, 1976.

Wiersbe, Warren W. **Be Confident (Hebrews).** Colorado Springs, Co.: Chariot Victor Publishing, 1989.

STUDY GUIDES

Swindoll, Charles R. **Christ's Agony and Ecstasy.** Fullerton, Ca.: Insight for Living, 1982.

TAPES

Hardman, Marlin. **Can a Person Be Sure?** Washington D.C.: Campus Crusade for Christ Conference, Date Unknown.

Swindoll, Charles R. **Why Hast Thou Forsaken Me?** Fullerton, Ca.: Insight for Living, 1982.

Swindoll, Charles R. **Post-Crucifixion Phenomena.** Fullerton, Ca.: Insight for Living, 1982.

Swindoll, Charles R. **The Peril of Falling Away.** Fullerton, Ca.: Insight for Living, 1983.

MP3

Hopper, Phil. **The Most Controversial Verses in the Bible.** Lee's Summit, Mo.: Abundant Life Baptist Church, 2013.

Printed in the United States
by Baker & Taylor Publisher Services